An Approach to
THE OLD TESTAMENT

An Approach to
THE OLD TESTAMENT

ROBERT MARTIN-ACHARD

Translated by
J. C. G. GREIG

1965

OLIVER & BOYD
EDINBURGH & LONDON

OLIVER AND BOYD LTD.

Tweeddale Court
Edinburgh 1

39a Welbeck Street
London, W.1

This book is a translation of *Approche de l'Ancien Testament* by Robert Martin-Achard, Professor at the Universities of Geneva and Neuchâtel. It was first published in the Collection La Foi et la Vie in 1962. Editions Delachaux et Niestlé, Neuchâtel, Switzerland.

First English Edition   ...   1965

PRINTED IN GREAT BRITAIN BY
OLIVER AND BOYD LTD., EDINBURGH

In memory of
Pastor Paul Perret

Foreword

ALL concerned with the relevance of the Old Testament for religious life and thought today will find this little book of service. It is untechnical and easily read, yet behind it there stands up-to-date scholarship. Sunday School teachers and students of theology will both find it easy to master, and the appendices, hints for study and book-list enhance its merits as a text-book.

The translator wishes to thank a colleague, Rev. Jean B. Robson, M.A., Jordanhill College of Education, Glasgow, for a number of helpful suggestions though she is not of course to be counted responsible for remaining inadequacies.

Generally, but not always, Scriptural quotations have been taken from the Revised Standard Version of the Bible, copyrighted 1946 and 1952 by the Division of Christian Education of the National Council of the Churches of Christ in the United States of America, and used by permission.

J. C. G. G.

Introduction

THIS work is intended for all who find themselves perplexed, repelled or even offended by the Old Testament; it is not therefore addressed to specialists but rather to those numerous faithful church people who do not understand that for Jesus and for the early Church alike the books of the Old Covenant made up all there was of the Bible.

These few pages that now follow are not claimed to be anything more than a first introduction to the Old Testament. They do not affect to remove every difficulty or dispel every obscurity. Their aim is to provide items of information in orderly fashion about various aspects of the Old Testament and thus to make it easier to understand. Those who wish to dig deeper will find the bibliographical material at the end to be helpful.

The plan and contents of the volume reproduce the substance of a course given in the spring of 1961 at the *Centre protestant d'études* in Geneva, under the title " L'Ancien Testament, cet inconnu ".

Contents

Chapter | | Page

FOREWORD | vi

INTRODUCTION | vii

I DIFFICULTIES IN REGARD TO THE COMPOSITION OF THE OLD TESTAMENT | 1
  Composition of the Old Testament | 4
  Completion and Transmission of the Old Testament | 9

II THE GEOGRAPHICAL AND HISTORICAL SCOPE OF THE OLD TESTAMENT | 14
  Introductory | 14
  Geographical Scope | 16
  Historical Scope | 24

III THE ARCHAEOLOGY AND THE LANGUAGE OF THE OLD TESTAMENT | 33
  Biblical Archaeology and History | 36
  Biblical Archaeology and the Texts | 38
  Biblical Archaeology and Religion | 41
  The Scope of Biblical Language | 43
  A concrete language | 46
  A complex of relationships | 48
  A creative Word | 49
  Time as an effective force | 50

IV THE OLD TESTAMENT MESSAGE | 52
  God with us | 55
  Living as the People of God | 58
  The Divine " Nevertheless ! " | 62

ix

Chapter	Page
V ON READING THE OLD TESTAMENT	66
" Atomistic " Reading	68
" Historical " Reading	71
Typological Reading	74
Theological Reading	77
APPENDIX I: CHRONOLOGICAL OUTLINE OF THE HISTORY OF THE CHOSEN PEOPLE	82
APPENDIX II: OUTLINE OF THE GROWTH OF THE OLD TESTAMENT	87
APPENDIX III: SOME MANUSCRIPTS OF IMPORTANCE FOR ESTABLISHING THE OLD TESTAMENT TEXT	90
APPENDIX IV: SOME PRACTICAL SUGGESTIONS	92
BIBLIOGRAPHY	95

I

Difficulties in regard to the composition of the Old Testament

THE dominant impression made by the Old Testament on its readers is of remoteness. The books that make up its contents, from Genesis to the prophet Malachi, introduce us to a world that is foreign, not to say bizarre.

Our piety is not by itself of any avail against this feeling of having lost our bearings: the geographical and historical setting of the Old Testament, its general appearance, its vocabulary and its content—none of these things brings it really close to us.

Our first task is therefore to recognize and reckon with the gulf that separates us from it.

Remoteness . . . We must take the word literally, with its reference to space. It will be sufficient to recollect that several thousands of miles lie between us and the regions where the nation most intimately associated with the Bible lived: now, between the West and the Near East, these miles account for an accumulation of differences in climate and vegetation, and therefore in ways of living and thinking. What does the inhabitant of our modern cities have in common with the Bedouin who, like Abraham, leads his flock from one pasture to another; and how are we to understand the importance of water for the native of Palestine if we have never seen for ourselves the barren steppe-land that seems to threaten this land of his which it surrounds ? The slightest rain, the tiniest spring, the dew itself, are precious pledges of life in a country preyed upon by drought: many are the scriptural statements that can be explained by this circumstance which the climate of Palestine forces upon men's attention.

The Promised Land, with its mountains and plains, its passes and its frontiers, to all of which the Bible makes constant reference, remains for most of us a mysterious, almost unreal region—for all too few have been those privileged to scale the slopes of Carmel or visit verdant Galilee or traverse the desert of Judah.

Remoteness is a word applying also to time, and this too must not escape us. Twenty or thirty centuries or more separate us from Biblical history. What has become of the Assyrians and Babylonians who with their bloody deeds and arrogant, ambitious claims filled the stage in Isaiah's and Jeremiah's day ? The name of Nebuchadnezzar, conqueror of Jerusalem, may awaken in us no more than the vaguest of recollections, if any. Hittites, Sumerians and Amorites are known to few save the specialists ; and as for the Philistine cities, the Phoenician ports of Tyre and Sidon, or the little states of Ammon, Moab and Edom, mentioned over and over again in Scripture, all these we cannot place either in time or in space. To understand the Old Testament must we really know the campaigns of Tiglath Pileser III or the victory of Pharaoh Necho I over Josiah at Megiddo—not to mention the Hyksos invasion and that of the Peoples of the Sea ?

Remoteness . . . a new difficulty arises from another angle. Our mentality is hardly at all in tune with that of man as we find him in the Bible; our modern secular way of thinking and living in the West seems incompatible with the oriental tendency to think in mythical terms, which characterised the " People of God ". Israel encountered God everywhere and lived as part and parcel of an eminently religious world ; our scientific universe secularises reality ; machines and statistics have no use for God. Our question is " Where is God ? ", whereas the Psalmist knows that he cannot escape Him (Ps. cxxxix). Because we belong to a different world, Bible words do not mean the same to us as they did for the Old Testament. We use the same vocabulary, but do not speak the same language and are not agreed on the sense of such everyday terms as " flesh ", " soul ", " heart ", " heaven ", " justice ", " love ", " peace " . . .

Remoteness is again the keyword in respect of another obstacle: the Old Testament is not an ordinary book which is read from the first page to the last: it is composed of different portions and contains repetitions, divergences and even contradictions. How can we avoid being struck by certain differences of form and substance ? What a contrast there is between the first chapter of Genesis and the narrative that follows ! And how are we to reconcile Ecclesiastes with the rest of the Old Testament as a whole ? Job is indignant at what the Wise Men of Israel accept without difficulty. Chronicles repeat the history of Kings without always agreeing with their source. And how many varieties of prophetic oracles are to be found ! It is not easy to find a guiding thread in this accumulation of disparate traditions: the composite character of the Old Testament sometimes discourages those who read it.

Remoteness, too, is the word where the contents of the books of the Old Covenant are under discussion. In them we hear a great deal about the God of hosts, about battle-cries and massacres and calls to vengeance . . . matters hardly compatible with the attitude of Christ who intercedes on the cross for his executioners and, in the Sermon on the Mount, asks his disciples to pray for those who persecute them. The Hymn to Love (I Cor.xiii) is on a different level from the song

3

of Deborah who sings of the ghastly end of Sisera (Judges v). The Israelite believer aspires to a terrestrial bliss (Ps. CXXVIII), whereas Jesus proclaims the Kingdom which " is not of this world ". The Beatitudes are hard to reconcile with the doctrine of strict retribution as it is understood by Ezekiel and his school.

In the eyes of many the Old Testament looks like a preparatory stage of the Revelation, now superseded since salvation by faith has followed obedience to the Law. At most the role of the Old Testament is (so we are told) to demonstrate the superiority of the Christian message; and to read it is superfluous—not to say dangerous, where it might lead the Church to put the clock back.

We have given an indication of some of the difficulties to be found in reading the Old Testament. This book, remote enough as it is on account of its geographical and historical setting, becomes all the more foreign when we think of the complexity of its composition, the peculiar mentality it reflects and the limited perspectives of the message it passes on to us. In the studies that follow we shall come back to these various points, hoping thus to ease the work of readers of Scriptures as they come to the Old Testament.

Composition of the Old Testament

Two facts govern the problems of Old Testament origins: (a) not a day but a thousand years or more was necessary for its composition; (b) like the New Testament, the Old Testament does not properly speaking constitute one book—it is made up of a collection of writings and with good reason Scripture was formerly called *ta biblia* (i.e. " the books "), thus accenting the plurality of the biblical documents.

We find, then, that the Old Testament is a kind of library of twenty-two books according to the Jewish tradition, twenty-four according to the Protestants, and forty-five for the Roman Catholic Church. Of these books the earliest elements go back well beyond the age of David (*ca.* 1000 B.C.) and the latest date from the second or the first century before the Christian era.

This collection, composed of works varying in importance and style and written at various times in the history of Israel with appreciable differences of religious outlook, lived and grew with the People of God. Holy Scripture is not a book written by God himself; it did not fall from heaven a finished product; and it is not a divine opus free from all trace of erasure; for God made use of men—of their languages, their words, and their fingers, and also of their qualities and their failings—in order to pass on to us his Revelation; his Word never comes to us save through instances of human experience and human literature.

But there is no question of regarding the Bible as the simple juxtaposition of a certain number of writings, put together after a fashion as circumstances dictated. The Old Testament was born and developed together with Israel and in Israel's bosom. It is as it were a living library undergoing constant revision as the centuries went on; it is in A. Gelin's words " a text on the march ", at one and the same time deciding what was to be the life of the Chosen People and reflecting their history and their faith. It is the echo of a tradition to which it both gives direction and affords sustenance.

Given a better knowledge of ancient literature and especially of the way in which gradually the various biblical books were put together, we are enabled to note that Scripture is made up of successive layers, of constant reappraisals and of additions which witness to its being for Israel the living Word of God, from the period of the Kingdom to the Roman occupation. Each generation has contributed its share to the whole; each century has sealed it with its own imprint. The people of

God at the same time carefully preserved their inheritance from the past and reassessed it in the light of the present; the Old Testament is the fruit of a tradition transmitted in faithfulness and interpreted with freedom—and we see it in its dominant lines and with its successive enrichments as a living organism whose manifold elements are for all their diversity interlinked and remain inseparable. Its repetitions, its tedious passages and even its contradictions—in short the whole complexity of the books of the old Covenant—then take on their full meaning; it neither astonishes nor offends, for it witnesses to the fact that the Old Testament is the outcome of a long history which it shares with Israel.

The different parts making up the Old Testament evolved on more or less parallel lines. The Pentateuch, that is, the first five books—Genesis, Exodus, Leviticus, Numbers and Deuteronomy—was shaped by diverse traditions the range of which it is the special business of the specialists to determine, together with their origin and their literary and religious characteristics. The earliest elements of the Pentateuch must to be sure have been stories, more or less lengthy, which would be repeated from one generation to another and would recall the destiny of certain great patriarchs, and that of famous cultic centres (Qadesh, Bethel &c.) or explain the origin of a rite, such as the feast of the Passover, or of a proper name such as that of Bethel. Later, the priests grouped around the sanctuaries, collected these oral accounts, organized them and attended to their proper transmission. Thus for a sizeably long period an important part of the Pentateuch will have been preserved thanks to oral tradition.

This does not cease with the appearance of the first texts—which, after the fashion of the Sumerian, Hittite or Babylonian legal codes, were probably documents of a juristic kind. The Decalogue[1] and the so-called Covenant Code

[1] In a different form from that in which it appears in Ex.xx (cf. Dt.v).

6

(Ex. xx–xxIII) belong to the oldest strata of the tradition, perhaps even to the Mosaic period.

With the establishment of the monarchy and the glorious age of David and Solomon, this literature underwent an important development. In the tenth century B.C. the earliest collections of Psalms and probably also of the proverbs took shape. An unknown writer composed at this time a notable history of the reign and family of David (II Sam. IX–xx; I Kings I–II). In regard to the Pentateuch, an experienced theologian composed the first great synthesis of sacred history, beginning with the creation (Gen. II–IV), and, by way of the election of Abraham and the deliverance from Egypt, ending with the occupation of the promised land. This collection, called "J" (Jahvist) [2], was written in the Kingdom of Judah and according to a recent hypothesis is likely to have been developed from an old ritual creed recalling the different stages in the history of the chosen people (Deut. xxvI.5–10; Jos. xxIV.2–13). Another synthesis, perhaps more recent and less important, is called "E" (Elohist) [3]; of it we have only extracts. It was probably composed in the northern Kingdom (Ephraim). In the seventh century a new tradition emerges in which the constitutive element is "D" (Deuteronomy), a kind of meditation or exhortation based on the Law, and reminding Israel of her *raison d'etre* in an age that was distressful for the chosen people as a whole. Deuteronomy will have been one of the decisive elements of the "deuteronomic" reform imposed by King Josiah in 622 B.C. After the exile, in the fifth century, probably under the influence of Ezra the Scribe,

---

[2] From Jahweh, the special name for Israel's God, which appears at the beginning of the narrative.

[3] Elohim (God) was used by the author till the point at which God revealed his special name to Moses (according to the tradition)—*e.g.* Gen. xxII.

the priests exiled in Babylonia worked up the document known as " P "—the " Priestly Code "—which, besides a whole series of laws that are in great measure cultic [4] contains a grand fresco of sacred history, beginning with creation (Gen. I) and tells of the series of covenants God sealed with Noah, Abraham, Moses and the priesthood.

It is generally thought that after being united the traditions J and E were completed by D and then by P in order to constitute about 400 B.C. the Pentateuch or the Torah (*i.e.* " the Law ").

The historical and prophetic books as also the Wisdom literature and the poetic books had a very similar fate. Oral and later written teachings were subsequently collected into units of much greater dimensions; successive generations who transmitted them were responsible for their completion; and their explanatory glosses reveal their historical and religious preoccupations.

Among the historical syntheses mention must be made of a narrative of deuteronomic inspiration, dating from the exile and now distributed among the books of Joshua, Judges, Samuel and Kings; and of the work of the Chronicler (fourth century B.C.), comprising the books of Chronicles, Ezra and Nehemiah.

The prophets, often wrongly called writing prophets, were first and foremost preachers, whose activity among their people was more in what they said than in what they wrote. It was usually their disciples who took the trouble to collect their oracles, and to arrange, annotate and transmit them. At times we can discern from their books the existence of collections of varying importance: thus in Isaiah v we have a group of apostrophes introduced by " Woe to . . ."; in Amos I and II diverse words of judgement are found with the formula " For three transgressions . . . and for four "; in

[4] *e.g.* the Holiness Code: Lev. XVII–XXVI.

Isaiah vi–ix there are several interventions by the prophet in connection with the Syro-Ephraimite war. Generally speaking the prophetic works are made up of all sorts of declarations: a disorderly sequence of invectives, appeals, promises, etc., which can most suitably be examined as separate items.

The Old Testament presupposes a gradual elaboration of most of the books that make it up. The Psalms, Job and Proverbs also have their special histories. But despite so much variety, the books of the Old Covenant are a whole, not an artificial assemblage of ill-fitting documents. If this is so, it is because all these writings belong to the one people and concern the same God; each of these texts in its own special way is a part of sacred history. The evident diversity of the pages of the Old Testament is no barrier to our recognizing their basic unity; all of them reflect the manner of their composition.

Completion and Transmission of the Old Testament

The Old Testament grew along with Israel; in a way it remained a live text transmitted by a tradition which constantly added to it; so it comes about that the Mishnah and then the Talmud, completed about A.D. 500, preserved and filled out its teaching.

However, round about the beginning of the Christian era, the Jewish authorities thought it necessary to fix the number of books that " soil the hands ", *i.e.* that are recognized as sacred. In this connection we have to state explicitly: (*a*) that the Old Testament canon, *i.e.* the text of books declared to be " sacred ", was not definitively closed when the Church came into existence; (*b*) that canonical (*i.e.* regulative) authority is unevenly distributed throughout the Old Testament.

As is shown by the prologue to Ecclesiasticus (written

9

about 132 B.C.) [5] and by the Gospel of Luke, the Jews distinguished three collections among the books of the Old Testament: the *Torah*, comprising the Pentateuch; the *Prophets*, with on the one hand the books of Joshua, Judges, Samuel and Kings and, on the other, Isaiah, Jeremiah, Ezekiel and the twelve minor prophets—making, say, eight books in all; and finally the *Writings*, or *Hagiographa*, among which are, notably, the Psalms, Proverbs, Daniel, Job, &c. This gives a total of 22 books (sometimes said to be 24), according to Josephus, the Jewish historian of the first century A.D.

The *Torah*, completed in the fourth century B.C., and associated with the great name of Moses, had at this period acquired an unchallengeable authority; it is the source of biblical revelation. The Samaritans considered it to be the sole canonical authority. The second group of writings were not held in such great esteem as that. It must have been gathered together at the time when Daniel, a book not counted among the Prophets, was composed. Discussions about the canonicity of the Writings went on for a long time—especially in regard to Proverbs, Song of Solomon, Esther and Ecclesiastes: a Jewish synod which met at Jamnia in A.D. 98 admitted them to the Palestinian canon, though the problem was not thereby definitively solved for all that.

Alexandrian Judaism was more flexible than that of Palestine, and both used and disseminated works like the Books of the Maccabees, the Wisdom of Solomon, Ecclesiasticus, Judith, Tobit &c.

Thus the Church did not inherit from Judaism a precisely defined canon; for long she herself was hesitant about the precise number of the canonical books; and an oecumenical decision was never taken on this point. The New Testament seemingly makes no explicit use of the Alexandrian

[5] Also known as the *Wisdom of Ben Sira*.

documents; contrariwise, it manages to utilise writings now rejected by the Church, such as the Ethiopic *Enoch* (see the Epistle of Jude). In Asia Minor the Fathers for long contested the authority of Esther and that of the books used in hellenistic Judaism, which Rome had no difficulty in admitting. The official standpoint of the Roman Catholic Church goes no further back than the Council of Trent (1546) which establishes the authority of the Alexandrian books.[6] The Lutherans and the Anglicans regard the Books of the Maccabees, Judith, Tobit &c. as being of an edifying character, but not as normative for the Church. The Reformed Churches are more reticent about them, without going so far as to exclude them altogether. It was customary for several centuries on the continent of Europe to print the Apocrypha at the end of Protestant Bibles in small print; unhappily in the nineteenth century the Bible Societies abandoned this tradition which had allowed the faithful to get to know works with a religious and also an artistic import-ance which was formerly very great.

From this rapid general survey there stands out the fact that the Church was never unanimous, any more than were the Jews, about the exact limits of the Old Testament. There is nothing disquieting in this for in things essential there is agreement: the authority of the Torah, the Prophets, and works such as the Psalms and Job was never in dispute. The margin of uncertainty which remains in regard to the closing of the Canon is precisely what forbids us to identify Holy Scripture in almost mechanical fashion with the Word of God. The Old Testament does not call us to believe in *it*, but to believe in Him to whom it bears witness both in its diversity and in its unity.

It remains to recall briefly what became of the Old

[6] These are often called " deuterocanonical " by Roman Catholic theologians, and " apocryphal " by Protestants.

Testament after its completion. The scribes, called Massoretes, jealously guarded the Hebrew text of the Old Testament. In the first few centuries of the Christian era they did not any longer rest content merely with carefully reproducing it; they worked out a vowel-system and a scheme of punctuation which makes it easier to read, and they noted all the peculiarities of Hebraic tradition in order to ensure as exact a transmission of the text as possible. Though its results were not perfect, their great industry claims our gratitude; thanks to the Massoretes we are enabled to read a Hebrew text which is not substantially different from that which Jesus knew and contemplated. Taken as a whole the recent discoveries of manuscripts at Qumran have confirmed the seriousness of purpose with which they went to work.

From the third century B.C. onwards there began to appear Greek translations of the Torah and then of the Old Testament with an eye to the Jewish circles scattered about the Hellenistic world. One particular result of this was the famous Greek version called the " Septuagint ", a production of uneven value, but one to which the Fathers accorded very great authority and which the New Testament writers generally employed. Among other translations we must mention (a) the Targum, a sort of paraphrase of the Hebrew text written in Aramaic for the use of the Jews of Palestine and Mesopotamia; (b) the Latin version known as the Vulgate, produced by Jerome and finished in A.D. 405, which had a mixed reception before becoming, after several revisions, the official text of the Roman Catholic Church, and (c) the Peshitta (=" simple ") version, written in Syriac, a derivative of Aramaic, and used by the Christians of Edessa in Mesopotamia.

With the help of Hebrew, Greek, Latin, Aramaic and other manuscripts that have escaped the ravages of time and the violence of men, specialists today are striving to reconstruct the primitive text of Holy Scripture.

We may in conclusion call to mind the names of some more recent translations: there was that of Luther, begun in 1521, for the Germans; there was that of Olivetan (a cousin of Calvin's), published in 1535 at Serrières, near Neuchâtel, for those of the Reformed Churches, and later revised by the Reformer himself; and we may list also the following:

Geneva (1560)
King James Version (1611)
Revised Version (1881)
American Standard Version (1901)
Revised Standard Version (1946–52)
New English Bible (N.T.) (1962)
In Germany—Menge (1926 O.T. 1909 N.T.)
In French, Louis Segond's Protestant version appeared
   in 1874, and the so-called Synodal Version in 1910.

Since the second war perhaps the most notable of several enterprises are the *Bible du Centenaire* (1947) and the Roman Catholic *Bible de Jérusalem* (1956).

It is proper here to note the tremendous work of biblical translation and distribution undertaken in the last 150 years by the Bible Societies whose constant endeavour is to make Scripture better known and to provide new translations of it, thus permitting everyone to read the sacred text in his mother-tongue and making possible the discovery of the Old Testament by the peoples of Europe, of Asia and of Africa.

II

The Geographical and Historical Scope of the Old Testament

Introductory

OUR interest in the historical and geographical setting of the Old Testament does not stem from mere curiosity about a remote region or past period. We are not concerned just to traverse a territory or go backwards up the stream of time; our preoccupation is theological and based on the fact that everything with a bearing on the Biblical revelation retains a decisive importance for the Church right through its history.

The spatial and temporal setting of sacred history are on the same level as the election of Israel and the person and work of Christ. Holy Scripture underlines the unique role of Jesus of Nazareth, Israel's Messiah, the one mediator between God and men (I Tim. II.5) in whom God intervenes to reconcile the world to himself (II Cor. v.19), *i.e.* the one name given among men for their salvation (Acts IV.12). Now the Christ belongs to Israel, was born in and of Israel, is Israel's Messiah and in his work confirms the apostolic pronouncement that salvation comes from the Jews. The presence of Christ in the midst of his people proves the election of Israel and the promises made to her by God. There exists a close relationship between the appeal addressed to Abraham at the beginning of sacred history and the birth of Jesus at Bethlehem—between the covenant at Sinai and the death of Christ on the cross. The uniqueness of Jesus the Christ refers us to the unparallelled role of the people which prepared his coming.

But in choosing Israel, God chose also a language, a land, and a time: a language which was to be the sacred language, a land which was to become the holy land, and an extent of time which was to constitute sacred history. The geographical and historical scope of the Old Testament in particular and of Holy Scripture in general are integral to the election of Israel and of its Christ.

Here we are coming up against the mystery of the Divine election which again and again baffles and even irritates us. Why this particular language or land or time? Why this people and that man?

How much simpler it would have been (so we argue), and how much more rational, for God to reveal himself at all places and all times, and thus swell the numbers of the faithful . . . but here we find the biblical message opposing this easy natural method by the claim of the uniqueness of Christ and his people, implying at once the " election " of Hebrew, of Palestine, and of the centuries that went by between Abraham and Nero. . . .

But God's choice is not exclusive: it has to do with the whole universe. God begins by separating, the better to gather together. Christ comes to save humanity; Israel is chosen to become a source of blessing for all nations (Gen. XII.3). The language of the prophets is " called " to be the sacred tongue of all believers; the holy land, today as previously, concerns the entire οἰκουμένη, or inhabited world; sacred history determines the course of universal history.

Our salvation was prepared and accomplished on the soil

C

of Israel; our future is still tied up with the fate of Jerusalem.
There began with Abraham an adventure that has continued
down through the centuries and is now our concern, after
the patriarchs, the prophets, the psalmists, and so many
believers, known and unknown. The Holy Land is our land
too, and sacred history is our history; in devoting a few
pages to recall the geographical and historical scope of the
Old Testament, we are not primarily satisfying our intellectual
curiosity: we are going back to what constitutes the source
of our faith and our hope.

Geographical Scope

We must first notice the central position occupied by
Palestine on the map of the world. The Middle East is the
meeting-place of three continents—Asia, Africa and Europe—
that have played a decisive part in the history of mankind. In
the heart of the Middle East (Fig. 1) are two regions, Syria and
that which is our special interest—the land of the Amurru
was what the Babylonians called it; the indigenous inhabitants
spoke of it as the land of Canaan; to the Greeks it was Palestine; it was the Promised Land to Israel; and it is the Holy
Land of the Christians.

With the Mediterranean in the West and the desert in the
East, Palestine, together with Syria, constitutes a part of what
is called the "fertile crescent"—a strip of cultivable soil
stretching in an arc from the Nile Valley to Mesopotamia;
men, elsewhere forced to yield to the sea or to the desert, can
establish themselves on this unexpectedly hospitable terrain.
Palestine appears, then, like an indispensable link in a chain
joining the great empires of the ancient world. It is a
necessary intermediary between the four points of the compass
—a buffer state for which the Egyptians, the Hittites, the
Assyrians, the Babylonians, the Persians, the Greeks and the

Romans were all contestants . . . a land designed to be the prize in endless combats.

Even more than Palestine, Syria was to be involved in the great conflicts of history; the Mesopotamian conquerors were to seek to possess it in order to reach the sea; the Pharaohs were to occupy the territories south of the Lebanon to ensure their protection from invaders coming from the north; the minor states of the Middle East were for ever dragged into this struggle; and Israel like her neighbours was to be the victim of the repercussions of international politics.

Not far from Beirut there is a narrow pass called Nahr-el-Kelb, *i.e.* " Dog River ", where we rediscover the names of several great figures of ancient and modern history: Rameses II, at war with the Hittites; Shalmaneser III, the Assyrian contemporary of Ahab; Nebuchadnezzar, conqueror of Jerusalem in 587 B.C.; the emperor Marcus Aurelius in a later day; and Allenby, conqueror of the Turks in the War of 1914–1918.

This military route was also to be that for wares and for ideas. Syria, and to a lesser extent Palestine were natural meeting-places and centres of exchange. Egypt left there traces of her occupation; Mesopotamian civilisation made its inroads. With the Philistines the Aegean peoples established themselves in the south, and in the north the Hittites descended from Asia Minor to the borders of Palestine. The Persians were to take possession, and then, following the campaigns of Alexander the Great, the Greeks; finally it was the turn of Rome. . . . When the present century began, Palestine was in Turkish hands; then the British occupied it for a while; and today Arabs and Israelis contend for this land subjected to so many rigours by history.

The peoples who trod Palestinian soil left some of their treasures there: Thebes, Babylon, Nineveh, Ugarit, Athens

17

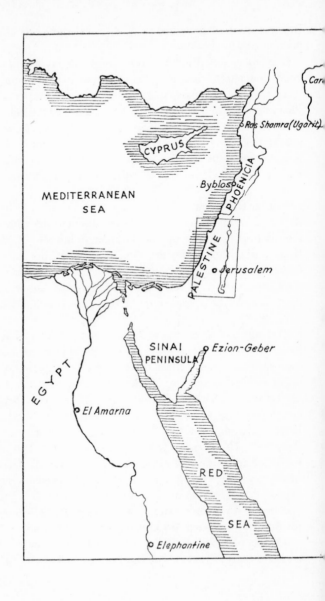

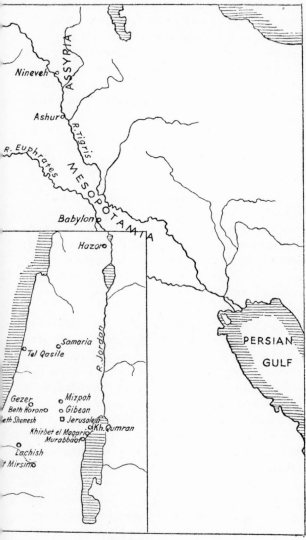

Figure I

and Rome among other pagan cities left part of their wealth there; the Old Testament has preserved the memory of these civilisations now buried in the sands.

If, with Syria, Palestine is a necessary intermediary between East and West, it is at the same time condemned to relative isolation on account of its own particular configuration. Syria allows the easy passage of troops and merchants; Palestine is hardly crossed by the great international highways. The region of Jerusalem in particular is not easily accessible and that ancient Jebusite city seemed to have to live on the edge of history because of its location. It required the conquest by David to make of it the holy city on which the gazes of believing Jews, Christians and Moslems converge.

Palestine (Fig. 2) forms a kind of quadrilateral some 160 miles long and 60-75 wide; its western frontier is formed by the Mediterranean, and on the east is the Syrian desert; northwards rise the mountain ranges of the Lebanon and the Antilebanon, and to the south stretch the Arabian steppes. The traditional limits of the country were Dan in the north and Beersheba in the south.

This relatively small territory is strikingly varied in its structure. It is composed of many fragments differing alike in vegetation and in elevation. It is parcelled out in little pieces in every direction. The Mediterranean coastal belt is narrow but fertile; in the north the Phoenicians built there important harbours like Tyre, Sidon and Byblos; the south for long remained in the hands of the Philistines occupying the cities of Ashdod, Gaza and Ekron. . . . The principal part of Palestine is formed by a broad strip of mountainous country dissected by passes and plains and comprising in particular (a) the mountains of Samaria (notably Mount Gerizim, 2849 ft.), (b) the mountains of Judah (more than 3000 ft.), (c) the plain of Jezreel, well-known for its vegetation, and (d) the Megiddo route, the strategic key to the country,

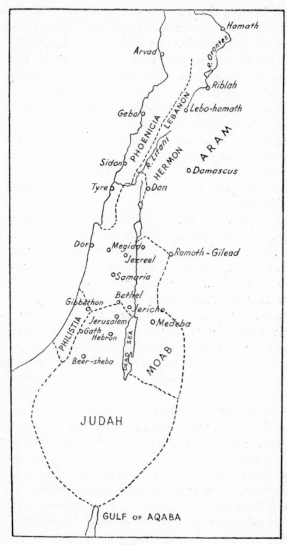

Figure 2

which has seen the march of the armies of Thutmose III, Necho II, the crusaders and Napoleon. More easterly is the renowned depression into which the Jordan flows. The river has its sources some 1000 ft. above the level of the Mediterranean, in green countryside, and runs through the Lake of Gennesareth to plunge in due time into the Dead Sea nearly 1300 ft. below sea level, in almost uninhabitable terrain. Beyond the Jordan the ground rises steeply to a plateau with fertile, well-watered soil, but on account of its remoteness Transjordan plays a secondary role in the history of Israel. She was to be constantly menaced moreover, by the Syrians and Ammonites in the north and by the Moabites and Edomites in the south.

Coming from the north we light first of all on the Sea of Galilee, of secondary importance for the Old Testament. This frontier territory, open to foreign influences and rich in manpower and in natural resources, is renowned above all as the setting of Christ's earliest preaching.

Further down there stretches Samaria, occupying a central position in Palestine. This is the region where the well-known sanctuaries of Bethel and Shiloh are to be found, as also the important towns of Samaria, Shechem and Megiddo and the principal roads linking Egypt with Mesopotamia. It is no surprise that in these circumstances Samaria had a troubled existence, especially in the period of the Israelite monarchy which, founded on Solomon's death, was to disappear under the assaults of the Assyrians (721 B.C.); nor that she has always been sensitive to foreign influences.

In the south, on the other hand, we have Judah, in an arid mountainous countryside, an unfriendly soil, favouring the development of an introspective kind of thinking and of an orthodoxy fiercely resistant to external pressures. Alongside Jerusalem the chief centres of Judah are Hebron and Jericho.

Palestine is a country of odd divisions, arbitrarily parcelled out and with no geographical unity, posing different and even divergent problems to the tribes of Israel. The period of the Judges reveals their particularism, while the revolt under Rehoboam is a witness to the clash between north and south. It is religious tradition alone that was to ensure a certain cohesion for the people of Israel.

It is appropriate to say a word about an entirely different aspect of the geographical scope of Scripture, in relation to the world as Israel knew it and the universe in which according to the People of God, sacred history unfolded itself. In accord with the conceptions of the nations surrounding him the Israelite generally divided creation into three: heaven, where God dwells, earth where man lives, and the nether regions, where the dead gather together. The God of Israel created the heavens and the earth: but his relationships to the world of the dead are hardly what one would call precise. That world seems to remain a secondary consideration in relation to the works of God and seems like a part—or an expression—of the primitive chaos overcome by God and banished by Him at the time of creation.

At the centre of the biblical universe is the earth, in the shape of a flat pancake (slab) resting on huge columns and everywhere surrounded by the waters which are the source of a fearful and oppressive threat to her. Indeed the waters also manifest the power of the original chaos; if heaven—a sort of celestial dome—holds them in check, then they are unleashed in the nether regions and as seas and rivers flood the soil.

Some traditions put the land of Israel at the centre of the earth, as the land of living beings *par excellence*, and in the centre of it the Holy City. Jerusalem is represented as the navel of the world—the vital centre of the universe, the rallying-point for all mankind—a sort of centripetal force summoning pagans to God's sanctuary (Isa. ii.2 ff.). (Cf. also Isa. xxv.6 ff; lx.i ff.; Haggai ii.6 ff.; Zech. xiv.i ff.; Ps. 87.)

This biblical geocentricism was for long accepted without any difficulty. Today it has lost any scientific character it had; but remains no less theologically pregnant than before. The universe as seen by Israel is in fact the expression of a faith she shares with the Church, even when the Church interprets it differently.

Historical Scope

The history of the Chosen People can de divided into three parts: (a) the period of the Hebrews, beginning with the patriarchs and ending with the entry into Canaan, from the eighteenth to the thirteenth century B.C.; (b) the period of the Israelites, from the age of the Judges to the disappearance of the State of Judah, from the twelfth to the sixth century B.C.; and (c) the period of the Jews, from the Babylonian exile to the wars with Rome, from the sixth century B.C. till the second century A.D. or alternatively with no ultimate date till, after centuries of dispersion and trials, the State of Israel was founded in 1948, the date marking the beginning of Israeli history.

The age of the Patriarchs. We have to concern ourselves with a decisive moment in the destiny of the People of God: the starting-point determinative of all that was to follow in Israel's development. From the strictly historical standpoint, this fundamental period remains obscure, for the relevant facts have only come down to us wrapped up in tradition. What made Israel what she became, set her apart as a " peculiar people ", and gave her a *raison d'etre* is recalled to mind by two names: Abraham and Moses.

24

According to the witness of Scripture, the ancestors of Israel belonged to the north of Mesopotamia, probably being in touch with important cultic centres like Ur and Haran. They are identifiable with the mass of Amorites or Arameans who led a semi-nomadic existence on the borders of the desert and sought to infiltrate into a more hospitable region. The traditions of Genesis, confirmed by recent archaeological discoveries like that of Mari, give an exact picture of the kind of life lived by the patriarchs who led their flocks from one pasture-land to another under the protection of a personal deity who guarded them as a faithful shepherd watches over his sheep.

It is hard to be more precise. Some historians place Abraham in the eighteenth century B.C. and make him a contemporary of Hammurabi, the great Babylonian monarch whose code today stands in the Louvre and who in particular vanquished the city of Mari, the ruins of which were discovered only some thirty years ago. The tablets of Mari allow us at all events to reconstruct a picture of the brilliant civilisation on the fringe of which lived Abraham and his descendants.

With Abraham the first chapter of sacred history begins. It opens characteristically with a promise by God answered by an act of faith. A wandering Aramean, addressed by God and in such a way that his subsequent existence is determined by this word spoken to him, paves the way for the existence of Israel.

A second moment is that of the liberation from the Egyptian yoke which leads up to the actual constitution of the People of God. The time of the Exodus is fundamental in the destiny and faith of Israel—it is the major event which heralds all the deliverances of the future; thus it is not astonishing to find it at the heart of Israel's creed.

The descendants of the patriarchs established themselves

in the Egyptian delta; their presence in the Pharaoh's country perhaps coincides with the invasion at the end of the eighteenth century B.C. by the Hyksos, pastoral peoples of Asian origin who were to be expelled by the XVIIIth Dynasty about 1560 B.C. Apparently an energetic king of the XIXth Dynasty who could be Seti I or his successor Rameses II (ca. 1300–1234) condemned the Hebrews to a harsh slavery. Under the leadership of Moses—whose name is of Egyptian origin—these people left the delta and miraculously escaped the monarch who was persecuting them. The Exodus will then have come to pass in the thirteenth century; guided by Moses the Hebrews came to dwell in the neighbourhood of Sinai and it is here that traditionally the Covenant was concluded between Yahweh the God of Israel and Israel the people of God.

From the very start God appears in Israel's eyes as the one who is not some force of nature but who is active in history and on account of this gives meaning to human destiny. The tie uniting Yahweh and Israel discloses the sovereign grace of God and his moral demands; the Decalogue, indeed, confirms Yahweh's saving act and lays down for Israel the way she must go if she is to preserve the life her God offers her.

It is the promise of Abraham and the Covenant, with the Law, concluded by the preaching of Moses which, filled out and developed and more closely defined, make up the essentials of Israel's faith and give direction to its whole existence. The nomad tribes snatched from Egyptian slavery were to share the same hope and be subjected to the same commandments. It was this common tradition, of which we may feel sure Moses was the prime mover, that was to make the Hebrew clans into the people of Israel.

It appears that the conquest of Canaan under Joshua's leadership—partial as it moreover was—is to be placed about 1225 in the time of Pharaoh Merenptah.

The Period of the Kings and Prophets. Once in the Promised
Land the people of Israel were an amphictyony, that is, a
confederation of tribes united by a common religious tradition. The political organisation of the chosen people was still
elementary; Israel was content to gather periodically round
the Ark, which was the visible symbol of God's presence in
the midst of his own, and from time to time she conducted
holy war under the leadership of some inspired personality;
for the rest, the tribes were organized to suit themselves.
The period of the Judges witnesses to troublesome anarchy
and loathsome immorality; the Israelites allowed themselves
to be contaminated by their Canaanite environment and were
indeed to a greater or less extent allied with the old inhabitants
of the country. In times of oppression and decadence, various
" saviours " arose and summoned the tribes to a holy war—
the most famous of them being Deborah, Gideon, Jephthah
and Samson. . . .

In the twelfth and eleventh centuries B.C. the Philistines
were a grave menace to the Israelites and Shiloh, where the
Ark was kept, even fell into their hands. To struggle against
the enemy a certain amount of centralisation proved to be
indispensable; Saul was therefore made King and achieved
some success. His successor, David, won a definitive victory
over the Philistines, was enthroned as king by the tribe of
Judah and then by those of Israel, and extended his sway not
only over all Israel but also over the surrounding peoples.

It is possible to speak about an empire of David. The king
conquers Jerusalem and by placing the Ark there he makes
the pagan city into the spiritual centre of the People of God.
His son Solomon was to build the temple that would confirm
the sacred character of Jerusalem. David, despite his weak-
nesses, remained in Israelite tradition the type of faithful
kingship, dear to the heart of God and of his people; thus
the Israelites came to desire as their ruler a new David; the

messianic hope is linked to the name and work of their greatest king.

Under Solomon Israel was to know a short period of glory and to be notably active in the domain of culture, but David's son was unable to prevent a schism. When he died the northern tribes refused to acknowledge his successor and appointed their own king, Jeroboam; the two states, warring brothers, were to go into rapid decline. The kingdom of Ephraim was practically never free of coups and revolutions— its instability was to hasten its ruin; while Judah, taking its stand in the Davidic tradition, was to have a less unsettled existence and to survive the disappearance of the northern state by some decades.

This period is marked by the conflict in which we generally find the prophet at loggerheads with the king and his people. The prophet intervened in the political sphere, protesting not only against an idolatrous form of worship or against social evils but still more against a way of conducting the affairs of state he considered to be incompatible with the religious tradition of Israel.

The prophetic preaching was not to succeed in bringing back the chosen people, and in particular its civil authorities, to the path of obedience and faithfulness.

In the kingdom of Israel one dynasty had a brief hour of glory in the ninth century B.C.—that of Omri, which was well-known beyond the bounds of Palestine. Omri made Samaria his capital; his son Ahab and his wife Jezebel, the Phoenician princess, came into conflict with the prophet Elijah while engaged in a struggle against the powerful Aramean state of Damascus. In the end the dynasty of Omri went down before their various enemies and Jehu had Ahab's relatives massacred and himself seized power; in the eighth century B.C. one of his descendants, Jeroboam II, secured for the Israelites a short period of peace and prosperity.

But the prophets Amos and Hosea rose up against the corruption which was prevalent in Samaria and throughout the country and proclaimed the imminence of disaster. The kinglets of Samaria were powerless to do anything against an Assyria at the height of its expansion, except to delay the evil hour. In 721 B.C. Samaria fell into the hands of Sargon II. The little state of Judah no more than escaped the same fate. Isaiah condemned the policy of Ahaz who was putting his faith in the Assyrian forces at the time of the Syro-Ephraimite War of 736 B.C., and he opposed the pro-Egyptian party who later tried to drag Hezekiah into a general revolt against Assyria (705–701). Hezekiah's successors were to be faithful vassals of the Assyrians to the point of introducing the official cult of their master at Jerusalem.

Assyria went down before the Babylonians and the Medes, in consequence of which Judah gained some respite; Josiah undertook a programme of political and religious reconstruction but unhappily died at Megiddo in 609 B.C. From then on the death pangs of Jerusalem began. Already in 597 Nebuchadnezzar had taken possession of it and deported part of the population. The weak Zedekiah yielded to nationalist pressure and sought to stand up to the Babylonians; Jeremiah and Ezekiel proclaimed that this was the end of Judah. The Holy City fell into pagan hands, the Temple was burned and the élite of Judah were deported (587 B.C.).

The period of the Law and the Apocalypses. Prophecy died out just after the Exile but not before it had claimed an audience for an extraordinary message of consolation from an unknown prophet called Second Isaiah (Isa. XL–LV) by the specialists. Cyrus the Persian conqueror reached Babylon in 538 B.C. and offered the Jews the possibility of returning to Jerusalem there to rebuild the Temple. This remained unfinished till 515, when the prophets Haggai and Zachariah intervened to good effect. The " Second

Temple " confirmed the role of Jerusalem as the Holy City for the whole of the Chosen People scattered throughout the entire Middle East.

In the fifth and fourth centuries B.C. Ezra and Nehemiah, both from the " Dispersion ", completed the political and spiritual restoration of the community grouped round the Jerusalem sanctuary; Nehemiah rebuilt the walls and restored the city to order, and Ezra imposed the Law on his Palestinian brethren: from then on Judaism was established, and was to resist the surrounding syncretism: it was to hold its ground despite persecutions and deportations, autos-da-fe and . . . gas chambers.

The Persian Empire grew weak and, following the victories of Alexander the Great, Jerusalem fell into Greek hands. Palestine was the object of disputes among his generals; turn about, the Ptolemies and the Seleucids occupied it. In the third century B.C. the Jews were relatively happy subjects of Egyptian rulers who looked with favour on their establishment at Alexandria. From 198 B.C. Jerusalem was a dependency of the Seleucids; one of them, Antiochus Epiphanes, sought to hasten the hellenizing movement which was traversing the whole of the Middle East and was beginning to reach the Jewish people; but he aroused increasingly active resistance. In 167 B.C. the crisis broke. The Jews accepted martyrdom, then took arms in defence of their faith. At their head were Mattathias and his sons, of whom the most renowned is Judas Maccabeus. The Seleucid forces were vanquished and an independent Jewish state came into being in 142 B.C. The heirs of the Maccabees founded a dynasty— the Hasmonean—but the Chosen People was divided, the Pharisees in particular going into opposition against the court. In the midst of intrigues and corruption Rome intervened, and Pompey took possession of Jerusalem by surprise in 63 B.C. A foreigner, Herod, succeeded in gaining recognition as king, reigning by subterfuge and cruelty. There were mutually hostile factions within Judaism: Sadducees, Phari-sees, Zealots, and Essenes. The Roman yoke became ever heavier and revolt and then open war broke out. In 70 A.D. Titus succeeded, not without difficulty, in entering Jerusalem; and in 132 A.D. a false Messiah, Bar Koseba (or Bar Cochebah) summoned the people to the struggle against Rome, and for three years held his ground against the legions of Hadrian.

This is the period of the priests and scribes who expounded, commented on, and adapted the Law, which was intended to determine every aspect of the life of the pious Jew. The aim of the Law (Torah) is to guarantee that the Holy God would have a people worthy of him: it is a " hedge " against sin and a protection against defilement. The responsible leaders of Israel took very seriously the vocation of their nation to be a people wholly consecrated to God. The attitude of the Pharisees in particular was to be exemplary in times of per-secution; there were to be countless martyrs to the faith during these harrowing centuries.

Alongside the Torah, the expectation of the Messiah, intensified by the sufferings of the Jews, was what character-ised the religious life of this period. The people lived in hope of seeing the final engagement between God's world and the demonic powers. The Gentiles would be humiliated, the impious punished, and Israel glorified on the day of the Messiah. Apocalyptic writings multiplied as a means of confirming the hopes of the faithful, and vied with each other in their descriptions of the stages of the catastrophe that was to precede the inauguration of the Kingdom of God. The Book of Daniel is one of these Apocalypses, and to the same category belong the Books of Enoch, the Assumption of Moses and IV Esdras. Communities came into being, more or less on the fringe of the official stream of

Judaism, possessing their own traditions, codes of law and apocalypses, as witness the documents found at Qumran.

In the midst of this political and religious ferment, in a profoundly divided nation that was bruised alike in its flesh and in its spirit, Jesus preached the Beatitudes, healed the sick and announced the coming of the Kingdom, dying for his people and for the world in the period of the Roman procurator, Pontius Pilate. A new page opened for the history of the People of God—but one not written in the Old Testament.

III

The Archaeology and the Language of the Old Testament

BIBLICAL archaeology is a science of which the astonishing
progress awakes growing interest in a huge public, as
witness the success of the various works devoted to it.
This is due to the fact that archaeology is a science of life, rais-
ing up before our eyes worlds buried in the sands and resur-
recting for us a humanity from which we are separated by
twenty centuries or even more. By means of *tells*, monuments,
manuscripts, papyri, ostraca and the thousand and one
objects not even noticed by the layman, a riddle is solved and
a chapter of the past is written—a new perspective is given
of the ancient world known to the people of the Bible.

Biblical archaeology has been in existence for a little more
than a century. It begins with the exploration of Egypt when
in 1822 Champollion succeeded in deciphering a hieroglyphic
text, and then turns to Mesopotamia and successively discovers
the Assyrian world with its conquerors, the redoubtable
Tiglath-Pileser, Sargon and Sennacherib (eighth century
B.C.); the civilization of Babylonia, with Hammurabi, the
lawgiver and warrior of the eighteenth century B.C.; and
finally Sumerian culture, till then unknown, with its tablets
of legislative, epic and " wisdom " literature belonging to
the third and fourth millennia B.C.

Yet other worlds arise before us: at the beginning of the present century the archaeologists excavated Boghaz-Kői, the ancient Hittite capital, in Asia Minor, and in 1929 Ras Shamra yielded the remains of a splendid Phoenician city, Ugarit; while in 1934 the town of Mari, destroyed by Hammurabi, emerged from oblivion.

Palestinian archaeology began at the end of the nineteenth century, without any such spectacular results at first. About 1880 there was discovered an inscription of the eighth century B.C. made by the workers whose task it was to excavate the tunnel of Siloam; in 1928 excavations laid bare important buildings of Solomon's period at Megiddo; and letters dating from the end of the kingdom of Judah were dug up in 1935 near the ancient Lachish. Recent researches at Jericho, Hazor, Gibeon, and Beersheba have yielded astonishing results. Mention should be made of the exploration of Qumran, subsequent to the discovery of the Dead Sea Scrolls. A series of expeditions has given us access to the remains of an important library which belonged to a Jewish sect of the Essene type, and among the documents recovered are all the books of the Old Testament except Esther. Best represented are Isaiah, Deuteronomy, Psalms and the Minor Prophets; and to the canonical texts must be added writings like the Book of Enoch, Jubilees, Ecclesiasticus, Tobit or again unpublished works among which are a series of biblical commentaries, a collection of hymns, the rule of the community, a treatise on war &c.

Biblical archaeology has led to the emergence of the Old Testament from its isolation. Up to the end of last century it was a world apart, a stray schist as it were, a document to be studied in and for itself, for lack of comparative materials. Today it is possible to place Israel's Scriptures in their historical, literary and religious setting; historians are able to verify what the Old Testament says thanks to the contribution of digs undertaken in the Middle East; literary critics can compare the pages of the Old Testament with the Egyptian, Sumerian, and Canaanite writings which we now have at our disposal: theologians can assess the scope of biblical affirmations by placing them in their religious context.

Archaeological discoveries are assuredly effecting a kind of Copernican revolution: the Old Testament no longer appears as mankind's oldest document: Hebrew is no longer the first language spoken by man; the People of God is no longer at the fountainhead of all civilisation. Countless writings preceded Holy Scripture; Israel appears late on the world's stage, while Egypt and Mesopotamia had already had a long and glorious history.

We must go further, and further indeed the specialists have gone. Many pages of the Old Testament send us back to earlier traditions: the biblical Deluge has Babylonian and Sumerian antecedents; Israel's Psalms recall forms used by the worshippers of Ra, Marduk or Baal; and the Proverbs of Solomon remind us of the pronouncements of the Egyptian and Mesopotamian sages. The originality of the Old Testament is then called in question, and so very soon is its truth. At the beginning of the century there raged a famous dispute on the theme "Babel und Bibel", some scholars making the claim—quite wrongly, to be sure—that the Israelites owed all their literature to the Babylonians.

Conversely various well-intentioned authors have seized on the results of Biblical archaeology to demonstrate the exactness of Scripture. The excavations of Jericho and Mari have assuredly verified many of the affirmations of the Old Testament, but its manifold problems are far from being solved; moreover, the truth of the biblical message cannot be based on so-called proofs supplied by the archaeologists. It is illusory to establish the credentials of a certainty dependent on faith upon the conclusions of science, which are always subject to revision.

Biblical Archaeology and History

Biblical archaeology allows us to place the Old Testament in its historical context. The information acquired by it gives us the chance of confirming this or that event reported by Scripture, or of setting Old Testament information in the framework of Middle Eastern history.

There are still many question-marks about the origins of Israel, but the discoveries of these last years have given us knowledge of the ancient world in the patriarchal period and the stories in Genesis sometimes agree down to details with what we otherwise know about the laws and customs of the semi-nomadic tribes living at that time. The exact date of the Exodus remains controversial but the descent of the Hebrews into Egypt is in the framework of movements of population such as that of the Hyksos, and the difficulties which the descendants of the Patriarchs encountered in the land of the Pharaohs can well have coincided with an effort at national reconstruction under an energetic ruler who could be Rameses II (ca. 1300-1234). The excavations of Jericho and Hazor have not yet allowed a solution of the problems raised by the entry of the Hebrews into Canaan, contrary to what some orthodox writers have affirmed.

Another series of witnesses makes us understand the immense danger run by the People of God in the eighth and ninth centuries B.C. at the time of the sequence of campaigns of the Assyrians in Syria and Palestine. From the time of Tiglath Pileser III (745-722 B.C.) the Assyrian troops were for ever in the region, pillaging, massacring and destroying. Conquered cities were given to the flames, prisoners impaled and populations deported. Damascus was taken in 732 B.C.,

Samaria ten years later; Ashdod fell in 711, and in 701 Jerusalem was saved only at the last moment.

The Books of Kings and Isaiah recall that terrible period and the Assyrian documents confirm their story. The rulers of Nineveh boasted of their successes. Shalmaneser III (959–824 B.C.) affirms his triumph at the Battle of Karkar (853 B.C.) over Ahab and his allies in these words: " I slaughtered 14000 of his soldiers. I swooped on them like Adad (the storm God) when he makes the rain pour down. I spread out their corpses everywhere . . . the plain was too small to let all their souls go down to the underworld. I used their corpses to help me cross the Orontes. . . ." This same ruler had Jehu, king of Israel portrayed on an obelisk kneeling before him offering him tribute.

Tiglath-Pileser III tells how he treated Menahem: " As for Menahem, I overpowered him. . . . He fled like a bird all alone and knelt at my feet. I imposed a tribute on him . . . and led captive his people and his goods ". Sennacherib boasts of taking forty-six cities from King Hezekiah, and of having expelled thousands of the inhabitants from Judah and made the King a prisoner in his residence " like a bird in its cage ". " I made his country smaller but his annual tribute to me bigger and bigger."

These declarations explain the hatred and horror awakened in the Middle East by the kings at Nineveh, and also the joy of the prophet Nahum when the Assyrian capital fell to the assault of the Medes and Babylonians in 612 B.C.

The attitude of the Assyrian conquerors also makes Isaiah's words stand out in striking relief; the prophet, in a bewildered Jerusalem, holds his ground against the enemy: his extraordinary calm is in contrast to the excitement of his people and of the entire Middle East at the approach of the invaders.

This example is sufficient to show us what meaning the biblical text can take on in the light of the documents won from the sands of Egypt and Mesopotamia. Sacred history, thanks to archaeology, becomes what it ought never to have ceased to be—a real history, written and lived through by men such as we are, located on our globe and not in some imaginary world. The clues taken by the specialists from sections of walls, from among fragments of pottery and even from pebbles, remind us that God writes out his plan of salvation for mankind through the agency of human creatures and not through angels. The biblical realism to which archaeology bears witness vouches for the genuineness of divine love towards men and prepares the way for the Incarnation.

Biblical Archaeology and the Texts

Biblical Archaeology allows us to place the Old Testament in its literary context. To be sure, Scripture does not have the appearance for us of a sort of *creatio ex nihilo*, since it is now plain that the Israelites borrowed profusely, directly and indirectly, from their neighbours. The People of God found itself at the crossroads of several civilisations and drew freely from the traditions of Egypt, Mesopotamia and Canaan. Countless Sumerian, Hittite, Egyptian, Phoenician and Babylonian texts can today be put side by side with pages from the Old Testament.

The Mosaic Laws have their parallels in the Assyrian, Sumerian, Hittite and Babylonian codes: the Psalms of repentance remind us of the prayers of the Mesopotamian penitents; Egyptian or Sumerian Wisdom Literature may have inspired the authors of the Israelite proverbs; Psalm 104 is comparable with the Hymn of Akhenaton to the sun; the story of the Flood is to be found also in Accadian and Sumerian versions. The prophetic pronouncements are reminiscent of the style of the seers of Mari.

These comparisons moreover do not call in question the uniqueness of the Bible message. Israel borrows but also transforms the material which the surrounding world supplied, in order to integrate it with her own traditions. What a difference there is between the majestic account of creation at the beginning of Genesis and the Babylonian epic about Marduk, the god who made the world with the body of the monstrous Tiamat whom he had, into the bargain, overcome only with difficulty! The Mesopotamian deluge is the outcome of the rivalry of the gods; in Genesis it is the result of human sinfulness.

The Middle Eastern texts discovered, translated and commented on by the specialists make it possible to throw light on obscure passages in the Old Testament, to explain some obscure formula, or to translate a text with greater accuracy than before. In the light of the discoveries at Ras Shamra, for example, the expression " rider of the clouds " applied to the God of Israel is no longer mysterious, since it was already used for the God Baal, a Canaanite vegetation-god (Ps. 68); in the same way the allusion to the Leviathan, the fugitive and twisting serpent of Isaiah XXVII, can be understood because of a text from Ugarit in which the God Mot addresses his rival Baal in these terms: " Thou hast smashed in pieces LTN (=Leviathan), the fleeing serpent, you will put an end to the powerful one with seven heads ".

But Biblical archaeology has favoured above all the study and knowledge of literary genres, their structures, their primitive life-situation and their evolution. Each text, no matter how ordinary, belongs to one particular literary genre, and if it is to be properly read this must be taken into account. We do not look for the same thing from a page of Shakespeare as we expect to find in the final edition of *The Evening Standard*; and a novel by Simenon and a work by Albert Camus are read on different levels. It simply is not possible to confuse an account of dogs dying of fever, Pascal's *Pensées*, a Biblical commentary, a play by John Osborne and a poem by Musset. In the ancient world, as now, documents show the existence of specific literary genres that have their laws and their *raison d'être*; so that an author's thought is not to be understood unless by putting his work in its correct literary niche.

In the last few decades the study of literary genres has made important progress, so that today it is a guiding light for the principal tasks of research. With the help of Egyptian, Mesopotamian, Phoenician and other literatures scholars have applied themselves to the task of defining the different styles used in the Pentateuch (narrative, myth, aetiological legend, legal texts, official lists, epics &c.), by the Prophets (oracles, exhortations, minatory pronouncements, autobiography, parable &c.), and in the other parts of the Old Testament.

In Israel's Psalter we now distinguish hymns, individual and communal laments, songs of thanksgiving, royal psalms and enthronement psalms, the songs of Zion, wisdom texts &c. This collection of prayers has come from the Jerusalem cult, the constitutive elements of which it is the endeavour of scholars to establish in detail. Formerly looked on as a late product of Jewish piety, witnessing to a legalist and individualist tradition, the Psalter expresses according to recent research the common faith of Israel in the period of the Monarchy. The lamentations do not, as had been thought, reflect the experience of a Jeremiah, but were composed by the Jerusalem priests for the benefit of the faithful coming to give voice to their wretchedness in the Temple. The songs of Zion are no longer regarded as expressing the thoughts of the Jews dispersed after the Exile throughout the East, but go back to Canaanite traditions about Jerusalem, the City of the Most High, which were integrated into the Israelite faith. Thus the study of the hymnology of the

Middle East helps us towards a better understanding of the prayers of Israel.

Speaking generally we may say that the literature restored to us by the specialists makes possible a knowledge of the Old Testament which is less bookish and superficial than previously; thanks to Biblical archaeology we have access not merely to texts but also to the inner life and intimate experiences of the peoples of the ancient world, as their myths, songs and legislation disclose them.

Biblical Archaeology and Religion

Biblical archaeology permits us to place the Old Testament in its religious framework. The Mesopotamian, Egyptian and Phoenician documents now collected have shown us the spiritual preoccupations of the Middle East when the Scriptures came into being. Thus we understand the kind of religious mentality Israel encountered, together with the pagan cults with which she was confronted and the rites and religious traditions assimilated or rejected by her.

Archaeology lets us see that the Israelite festivals have a long history going back to a period before the Old Testament in their origins. The Semitic holy places served as models for the Temple of Yahweh at Jerusalem: the cult in the Holy City was organised on the basis of non-Biblical traditions, yet here the Old Testament shows that Israel was not content just to borrow some such cultic practice but adapted it to her own perspective and thought it out afresh in relation to the special elements in her faith. So we find the Sabbath, originally observed, it may be, by the Babylonians, the Canaanites or the Kenites, acquired a unique significance in Jewish tradition: Deuteronomy associated it with the work of liberation accomplished by Yahweh for the Hebrews; and the priestly code wrote it into its account of creation in order

to make it have a bearing at once on liturgy and on eschato-
logy. The feast of the Passover has a long history behind it
too: it originates in the time when Israel's ancestors were
still a pastoral people; tradition later associates it closely with
the Exodus; and in the New Testament period it is the
principal Jewish festival, recalling and proclaiming God's
saving work.

Biblical archaeology also lets us see the temptations to
which the people of God were subjected by their contacts
with the religious traditions of the Middle East. Egypt was
dominated by preoccupation with the hereafter and funerary
rites had an important place there; Babylon appears as the
city of sooth-sayers, magicians and astrologers, the capital
of Marduk, the god whose solemn festivals brought together
thousands of the faithful annually on the first day of the year.
Canaan is characterised by the cult of the forces of nature,
with an appetite for enjoyment which found expression in
orgiastic rites such as sacred prostitution.

The Old Testament denounces the worship of the Baals
and Astartes and condemns Canaanite immorality, but the
Ras Shamra texts enable us to understand better the reason
for these traditions and their attraction for the Israelites. Baal,
the supreme divinity of life, assures the fertility of the fields,
and the fecundity of flocks and men, but he meets Mot, the
god of the ripe grain who evokes drought and death. Year
by year the struggle goes on between Baal and Mot: the
vanquished Baal descends to the abode of the dead in the dry
season and triumphantly rises again from it when the rain
is about to fall on Palestine. The purpose of the Canaanite
rites is to ensure Baal's victory, for this is proved to be
indispensable to men.

Canaanite worship is the religion of life: the cult of the life
force in its most elementary form. Israel, penetrating into
Canaan, encountered this religion. Now, the chosen people

came from the desert across which Yahweh had led them, and from then on found itself on soil of which Baal is the master. Why should they not worship the God of vegetation without abandoning the traditions of their fathers? Elijah vigorously protested against this sharing of worship and a century later Hosea again took up the struggle. Israel had to learn that Yahweh alone gave her life and that to him she owed the bread necessary for her existence. The God of Israel made a successful take-over bid for the territory of Baal, but without correspondingly becoming the expression of some force of nature and without consenting to follow the cycle of seasons which condemned Baal to descending each year into the nether regions. Elijah's struggle on Carmel and the pronouncements of Hosea gain fulness of meaning when we undertake an assessment of the importance of Baal-worship on the soil Israel inhabited.

Thus in showing us the religious atmosphere of the chosen people's environment Biblical archaeology assures us of a better understanding of the Bible's message.

The Scope of Biblical Language

It is common knowledge that the Old Testament was written in Hebrew except for some passages in Daniel and Ezra for which Aramaic was employed. From the time of the Exile onwards, Aramaic began to become the living language of the Jewish people. As for Hebrew, " one little daughter of the great family of Semitic languages " (W. Vischer), it belongs to the Western Semitic group, together with Canaanite, Ugaritic and Phoenician. It has been defined as follows: " a language rich in colours and with fine shades of meaning, eminently suitable for expressing the great experiences of life, for painting pictures with great vividness and for narrating tales with great expressiveness, yet without being particularly penetrating in its thought: a language of poets and prophets, not of thinkers." (H. Fleisch). Hebrew was set apart by God to transmit his Word to men: " it is the sacred language, the source of theology " in W. Vischer's phrase. Vischer recalls Luther's saying: " Theology is a kind of study of language, meaning that particular linguistic study which is concerned with the learning and comprehension of the words of the Holy Spirit."

Every Christian must have some acquaintance with the language of Holy Scripture: moreover he speaks it unawares, not only when he uses the term " Amen " but also because Hebrew has made a deep impression on the Greek of the New Testament. The apostolic writers crammed their writings with Hebraisms to the point of coining expressions unknown to classical Greek. These expressions passed from Greek into Latin and thence into the new translations in European, African and Asian languages, so much so that in certain respects Christians all over the world use a common language which is neither the Greek of St Paul nor the Church's Latin nor the English of the Ecumenical Movement, but simply the ancient Hebrew of Isaiah and the Psalmists!

The following are some examples of terms and formulae that come from this language chosen by God to transmit his Word to us: amen, cherubim, paradise, scapegoat, flesh of my flesh, the shadow of death, the tree of life, the Lord of hosts, to believe in God, to have mercy, to find grace, to stop one's ears, to transgress against the Law, in the name of God, etc.

A knowledge of Hebrew should be cultivated among us, since certain passages of Scripture lose their flavour, not to say their meaning, in a translation. The Old Testament contains all sorts of etymological or prophetic plays on words. Thus Genesis tells us that woman is to be so called because she has been " taken out of " man (II.23). Only by turning to the original language can we see the connection, since there we read that the woman is to be called *ishsha* because she comes from the *ish*. Amos teaches us in a vision that Israel is ruined; what he does is to contemplate a basket of ripe fruits (*ḳayiṣ*) which is a sign of the end (*ḳēṣ*) (Amos VIII.1 f.). Jeremiah sees a rod of almond (*maḳḳēl shāḳēdh*) which reveals to him that Yahweh is "watching over" (*shōḳēdh*) his word "to perform it" (RSV), Jer. 1.11 f.; Isaiah denounces his people's iniquity in the parable of the vine, finishing with a striking formula which does not have the same vigour in our translations: (Yahweh) looked for justice (*mishpāṭ*), but behold, bloodshed (*miśpāh*); for righteousness (*ṣedhāḳāh*), but behold, a cry (*ṣeʾāḳāh*)" (RSV), Isa. v.7. The same prophet confronts Ahaz and his subjects with the alternative of believing or perishing (Isa. VII.9); the Hebrew formula, which plays on the different senses that the term *amen* can have possesses a flavour which our versions do not pass on: *im lô taʾamînu, kî lô tēʾamēnu*. These examples are enough to show the value of placing our versions over against the original language of the Old Testament.

We must go further. The problem goes beyond that of translation. A language is more than a series of words, grammatical rules, declensions and conjugations. It is the expression of a culture; it reflects a mentality; it reveals the profound structures of a way of thinking. We cannot understand a person unless we have made ourselves familiar with his language; there can be no communication with a people whose speech we do not know. The matter is even more complicated with the Old Testament, since Hebrew does not belong to the Indo-European group of languages and is therefore peculiarly foreign to us.

It is moreover used by a people who lived in a religious world and whose mentality was prelogical; in some respects Hebrew is more open to the African or Asian than it is to the disciple (however distant) of Plato or Descartes.

45

We are therefore invited to undergo a kind of intellectual conversion when we open the Bible. We have to make ourselves into " spiritual Semites " as someone has put it. " In order to read the Bible " remarks a Catholic theologian (G. Auzou), " we have to think and feel as it does—as Semites, Israelites, Palestinians. This uproots us and obliges us to become reacclimatized, for we are not orientals."

The comparison has often been made between Greek thought, stemming from Plato, to which we remain indebted, and the Hebrew mentality. Moreover there has sometimes been a tendency to over-emphasize the opposition between Athens and Jerusalem by a process of sweeping over-simplifications; nevertheless the men of the Old Testament lived and thought in a world strange to Westerners. It is appropriate to underline here some of the characteristics of Hebrew thought.

A concrete language

Hebrew has very few abstract words. It has no terms to denote nature, matter or universe. It says " heaven and earth " to designate the world as a whole; to express God's creative act, unique of its kind, it cannot draw on the expression *ex nihilo* but suggests the fact by employing a series of expressions borrowed from the mythological terminology of Babylon (chaos, abyss, darkness etc.).

Words evoked attitudes, qualities and concrete situations for the Hebrew; even when their meaning has evolved and become richer they remain connected with their original sense. Some examples will illustrate the dynamic realism of the sacred language.

" Glory " implies something heavy and weighty; the man who is honoured has some " weight "; whence the Pauline expression " weight of glory " in II Cor. IV.7.

46

"Peace" is a reality definable not by the absence of struggle but positively, by plenty and abundance. It comes from a root which evokes the idea of something full or complete.

The "soul" is first of all the breath or respiration and its location—the throat; its meaning extends to life itself, of which it is a condition. The soul also designates the person and the formula "my soul" may be translated "my-self". To lose one's soul is therefore to lose one's breath and so one's life. The soul is, moreover, so little to be regarded as an immaterial, indivisible and immortal reality that we find it sighing, rejoicing, being impatient, quenching its thirst, trembling with horror . . . and dying. We must here beware of regarding it as the opposite of the body and the flesh, for to the Israelite man formed an indissoluble unity.

The "Spirit" is primarily the breath and the wind and retains this meaning: this connection of senses is apparent in Ezekiel's vision (Ezek. xxxvii) and in Jesus' teaching on baptism (Jn. iii).

"To liberate" comes from a root meaning "to make room". Deliverance allows a man to find all the space he needs for living.

The "enemy" on the other hand is someone who shuts one in, compresses one, or confines one in agony and drives one into a corner.

To "expiate" means, properly speaking, to rub out, to erase the blot, or, by another etymology, to conceal it.

"Being" for Israel implies more than mere existence: it is "becoming" "acting", "being effective" . . .

To our eyes Biblical vocabulary confuses the material and the non-material, the concrete and the abstract; it is astonishingly graphic in its imagery; it is living and realistic and requires to be understood on its own terms.

In the biblical perspective everything is involved in multifarious relationships; thus the terms used by the Old Testament are relative. They do not tell us what things are in themselves, but place them in relation to God and man. Genesis shows us human beings placed in a threefold relationship: towards the Creator, the creature, and the creation; seen in this perspective the " fall " signalizes first and foremost a breach of relationship.

One is struck by the number of juridical ideas used by the Old Testament: covenant, justice, judgement, law, grace, law-suit, witness, truth &c. Legal language expresses perfectly this fact of the Israelite's understanding existence on the basis of a constellation of relationships; in which it is appropriate to recognize their distinctive character and their essential unity. In particular the part played for Israel by the ideas of the covenant is well-known. In this we see that God's people does not conceive of justice apart from the framework established by Yahweh; whatever is just is so in relation to the God of Israel; right is conformity to the divine will clearly expressed in the law. The Pauline thesis of justification by faith can be understood thanks to this Old Testament idea.

One of the fundamental ideas of the Hebrew mentality is that of participation. Reality is constituted by a more or less implicit law, according to which the part is present in the whole and the whole in the part. All Israel is present in each of its members and every Israelite is a manifestation of the entire chosen people. A single individual represents the community, whether of the past or of the present or of future. Israel is the bearer of mankind's destiny in herself; Abraham does not belong to one human epoch but lives on in his descendants; every King of Judah is a son of David and a bearer of the Messianic hope; to smite the son for the father is not to commit an injustice, for the father lives in the son. The Israelite cult and legislation, and in particular the ideas of substitution and redemption, are based on the relationship established between the part and the whole, the people and the individual, the body and its members. That relationship does not have to be made explicit. The idea of participation has a theological bearing which is also relevant for the New Testament.

A creative Word

The Hebrew, sensitive above all to what he hears, turned even his visions into a Message, as the prophetic books testify. He described badly, but he knew how to listen. The Greek contemplated the world as if it were a play, and cultivated the sense of the beautiful and the sense of proportion; for him the universe was a cosmos, an ordered, harmonious whole. Israel was guided by the word, which was not Thought, but Event, it belonged to the sphere of action and of life. It was urgency, dynamism and effectiveness. When God speaks he creates; the prophet's pronouncement hastens on catastrophe or salvation; truth is something that is done, and wisdom something that is practised. To know is not only to observe and be aware of something in terms of one's rational intelligence; above all it is to encounter and participate in something—to listen and to receive. Knowledge implies a communion and involves the whole being.

The *name* was of first-rate importance for the Israelite; it explained the being to which it was attached; it determined his destiny and was the basis of his vocation. So it was with the biblical names Abraham, Israel, Isaiah, Jesus, Peter. Naming was an act of authority, and to know someone's name was to have power over him. Thus it was that Israel did not have the right to pronounce the name of Yahweh at discretion.

The existence of the chosen people was constituted by a dialogue between God and Israel with which all creatures were associated to a greater or less degree. One day the universe would tell of the glory of Yahweh; today he creates history by his Word, which becomes one with his interventions in history. The Exodus, the election of David, the victory over Midian, the Assyrian invasion, the elevation of Cyrus to the throne of Persia, were so many divine words marking off the various moments in the destiny of the people of God and of mankind as a whole.

Time as an effective force

The Greek lived in a harmonious space and was unsympathetic to the time factor. Time meant ageing, decay and disintegration. Everything passed away and dissolved on its account. Time led nowhere and salvation consisted in escaping from its clutches.

The Israelite created no works of art but he was involved in a history which was bound to reveal the rights of his God over the universe. He sought the honour of Yahweh rather than beauty and he accepted time as an instrument for the accomplishment of the divine plans. Israel's destiny was made up of a succession of days and moments to which God had given content and meaning, and it developed on a pattern of promise and of fulfilment of the divine word; it had a beginning and an end. To the chosen people time meant enrichment, the development of maturity and the fullness of flowering; it allowed the seed to grow and the tree to yield its fruit; it permitted the Kingdom of God to come. There was no question of fleeing but rather of living.

In this way the Old Testament invites us to take seriously

the most humble material realities in the world God has created; it is in fact by them that he indicates his presence to us. And our task is to discover this world of relationships and acts of participation in which we are involved; sin is always a breach of relationship—it is a rejection of one's neighbour—and life is acceptance of one's neighbour. We are united with former and future generations and with the most far-off peoples in an all-embracing solidarity. Biblical language makes us also pay heed to the true wisdom of letting God speak to us and guide us in a dialogue which reaches its fulfilment in the confession of faith; it reveals to us, finally, that time, which God has given us, is not something to be cursed but allows us to draw nearer to our goal, which is God himself; we are pilgrims journeying towards the Holy City and not vagabonds condemned to wander eternally. To sum up, we are not to be contemplating the God of the scholars and philosophers, but to be hearkening to the God of Abraham, Isaac and Jacob.

IV

The Old Testament Message

ERE we have to express in a few pages what is the essential content of the Old Testament; it is unnecessary to underline the difficulty of this undertaking. Is it even legitimate to claim to summarize a document with elements distributed over ten centuries and giving evidence of interests sometimes very diverse indeed?

It is however demonstrably indispensable not only to say what the contents of this or that writing are or to expound the meaning of a particular passage, but also to unravel the principal threads of thought in Israel's Holy Scriptures and show their central ideas. It is a question of recognizing the skeleton and the joints in what is a living organism.

But by what principles is such an account to be guided? What is to be the starting-point of an enquiry of this kind?

The specialists have debated which of several solutions to choose; one is to follow the plan of a systematic theology and tackle each of the great themes of dogmatics in its turn. The Old Testament will then be investigated for its viewpoint on the problem of God and his attributes, man and his destiny, history and the means of salvation; and there will be drawn from scripture elements that are relevant for the working out in detail of a doctrine of creation, atonement, or divine justice. This work, though not useless, overlooks the fact that the Old Testament came into being in the course of a history extending over more than ten centuries; it ignores the time factor and makes no distinction between affirmations to be found in different contexts. It is not surprising that Israelite thought should have been modified between the time of David and that of Ezra and it is not always easy to reconcile this or that pre-exilic pronouncement with the more recent Old Testament writings.

We must never forget that the Old Testament is not a treatise in systematic theology thought up by a western brain; it is the reflection of concrete experience. Its language is religious, not speculative, and it does not lay bare a certain number of truths about God, mankind and the universe, but relates a series of events which reveal the God of Israel. Justice is not done, for instance, to the theology of the Psalmists when we are content to record that they describe the greatness of the Almighty and tell of his anger at the godless man and his grace towards the pious; formulae of this kind fail to take account of the fervour of which the entire Psalter gives evidence and which also appertains to the biblical revelation.

To speak likewise of Yahweh's omnipotence, to underline his omniscience and omnipresence, to call to mind his eternity and immutability gives a false impression of the point of view from which the Old Testament was composed and is a betrayal of its authors' intentions. It is inappropriate to turn pages charged with passion and life into an abstract exposition that is ponderous with soulless verities.

Another solution is to take into account the historical factor which is of such decisive importance for Scripture and to be guided by chronology. It is then appropriate to investigate the various witnesses of Israel in their turn, and to group the texts according to the order in which they were written (pre-Davidic documents, works contemporary with the Monarchy, writings of the exilic period, literature of the post-exilic Restoration, etc.). This kind of presentation will show up the diversity of viewpoints and will amount less to a summary of the Old Testament message than to an account of the history of Israelite religious doctrines. We will be told, in turn, what was said about God and man by the deuteronomic or priestly school, by the prophets Isaiah or Jeremiah, or by the author of Job.

This way of exhibiting Scripture may do justice to the chronological framework in which biblical truth gains expression, but such truth is then in danger of disintegrating in a host of individual analyses and a diversity of pronouncements, all simply set down side by side without any means of showing the underlying unity. Now, the contents of the Old Testament are affected by the fact that its pages are all connected with a people involved with Yahweh in a common enterprise. A synthesis must be obtained without doing violence to history.

Within the framework of a theology of the Old Testament, some recent accounts arrange the content of Scripture around a concept taken from the examination of the sacred texts itself; we have sometimes underlined the importance of the idea of covenant or relationship in Israelite tradition; we have also drawn attention to the part played by history as sacramental in relation to the biblical revelation; and finally we have seen the progressive development of a cultic creed in the Old Testament. Yet it seems that no theology of the Old Testament succeeds in exhausting its riches. To say this should remind us that Israel's Scriptures are in a sense incomplete: the key to them is to be found beyond the canonical documents in the person and work of Christ who in response to the expectations of his people has given fulness of meaning to the pages that prepare the way for his coming. The lines that follow cannot claim to be more than a "tentative sketch", the aim of which is to emphasize certain dominant ideas in the sacred Scriptures of the Chosen People.

"God is": this affirmation is, according to one expert (L. Köhler), the "essential" gift of the Old Testament to humanity. Even the least attentive reader cannot indeed fail to be struck by this presence of Yahweh which is revealed in every sphere of Israel's life. God intrudes on his people at every moment in their history: he "is", that is to say he lives and acts; the pages of the Old Covenant bear witness to this, each in its own way, from Genesis to Ecclesiastes, from Deuteronomy to Job, from Isaiah to Proverbs, from the Psalms to Malachi. Yahweh asserts himself as Lord by each of his acts, whether he creates or destroys, saves or condemns, whether drawing nearer or withdrawing his presence, revealing or concealing himself; Israel has to reckon with him at every moment and no creature can escape him. The question of God's existence is not raised; it is only the corrupt fool, the Psalmist tells us, who dares to claim that "there is no God" (Ps. xiv). The questions raised by Job are those of the believer, and the "why?" of the Psalmist (Ps. xxii) is the expression not of incredulity but of faith.

God has authority over all beings and he, not man (as the sophist Protagoras would have it), is the measure of all things. He is the measure of his creatures and of his creation; nothing exists apart from what he has created; everything takes on meaning in relation to him. He is the Living One who imparts life, the Just One who is the basis for all justice, and the Holy One who makes holy.

The entire Old Testament confesses Yahweh's sovereignty; he is the unchallenged master of the universe and has authority over all the beings that people it. His glory fills all the earth (Isa. vi); II Isaiah proclaims him the First and the Last, apart from whom there is neither God nor Saviour (Isa. xliv.6).

In his sight a thousand years are as a day (Ps. XC), his word endures eternally though heaven and earth will pass away (Isa. XL; Pss. CII; CIII). The Old Testament has the sense of holiness, that is of the transcendence of a God who is no more a projection of men's dreams than he is made in the image of our mediocre selves.

The Old Testament is properly speaking a theophany—that is, a manifestation of God. It tells us of his revelation to Israel and through his people to the world. It declares to us that both all creation and each one of his creatures have as their chief end his glorification. History is made up of a series of "theophanous" words and acts by which Yahweh vouches for his divinity; it reaches its fulfilment in the Parousia, so that the universe will confess the greatness of the God of Israel which the faithful gathered together in the Temple at Jerusalem were already proclaiming in song (Pss. XCVI; XCVIII). This theocentric aspect of the Old Testament message requires emphasis; what is known as *Heilsgeschichte* (salvation-history) is essentially the plan God has made to reveal himself to the world. "They will know that I am the Lord (Yahweh)"; these are the words by which Ezekiel indicates the aim of the divine interventions. "All flesh shall know that I am the *LORD* your Saviour" (Isa. XLIX.26); thus "II Isaiah" shows that Israel's redemption is closely linked with the honour of the divine Name. "I am the LORD (Yahweh)" is the constant reminder of the Israelite Law (Lev. XVIII. 4, 5, 6, 21, 30), the obedience of the Chosen People being thus associated with the glory of their God.

However God does not appear in the pages of the Old Testament as the Supreme Being who is self-sufficient, but as the God who enters into relationship with his creatures, a God as it were with his face towards the world, coming to meet mankind. The God of the Scriptures does not jealously stand guard over his independence; he bridges the gap and establishes links between men and himself—he is the God of the Covenant.

The Old Testament tells of this visitation or, better, dwelling of God among men. Yahweh is " God-with-us " —Immanu-El—he establishes his tabernacle with his people, he speaks the speech of Palestine, he lives the history of the Hebrews, the Israelites and the Jews. His Presence is not merely apparent: he walks at the pace of human beings, he employs their stammering language and follows their uncertain route; he learns their words in order to teach them his Word. The anthropomorphisms, of which Scripture is full, and which surprise and offend more than the occasional isolated reader, bear witness to that great divine patience—to the schooling of a Father who wants to be understood by his children, to the wonderful faithfulness of a God who has made time to talk to men before his Word became flesh and dwelt among us, full of grace and truth (Jn. 1.14).

Yahweh offers his friendship without ceasing to be himself; he is the thrice holy God, and yet he adapts himself wholly to his people, such is the paradoxical affirmation of Israel's Scriptures. The Old Testament is in this regard the Book of the Covenant—or Covenants, since the Mosaic part is preceded and followed by other Covenants; Noah, Abraham and David are, along with Moses, Yahweh's associates; Jeremiah announces the conclusion of a new covenant that will achieve what the old was unable to accomplish (Jer. XXXI.31–34).

God lays his hand on Israel and makes a people of them. An important passage in Exodus (Ex. XIX) reveals Yahweh's intention: Israel will be his special property, his witness to the world; it is the priestly nation—the intermediary between the nations and the only God. The mediatory function of the chosen people is confirmed by II Isaiah when he declares that the Servant of Yahweh, by his existence among the peoples, testifies to the greatness of the God who has chosen him; the Holy One of Israel, to use Isaiah's expression, shows his holiness in setting Israel apart for himself. God links his name with the destiny of the children of Abraham; his revelation is in their hands and his honour depends on their faithfulness to their vocation. Israel's attitude is to lead the universe to sing the praises of Yahweh and it can have a diametrically opposite result if the chosen People shows itself unworthy of its mission. The Covenant is a wager God has made with Israel as the stake.

Living as the People of God

The question raised right through the history of Israel was this: will Yahweh's partner live in conformity to the Covenant? Will Israel really be the People of God? What will she make of the Word God has confided to her, of the Cult and the Law which clarify that Word, and of the promises that go along with it?

Israel's response to her vocation was the great unknown factor accepted by God, the risk he ran at every moment of sacred history, when he called Abraham, bound himself to Moses, chose David, raised up his prophets, sent Ezra and Nehemiah . . . and, lastly, his Son!

Israel had to accept herself as Yahweh's people and constantly to recognize her mission and take it upon herself. She had to live in this world as the holy nation of the Holy God. She remained free to reject her vocation, to be just one people among others, lost in the anonymity of the nations; and she could have cornered for herself the blessings with which Yahweh had entrusted her, making use of God instead of being used by him and regarding herself as the purpose of history instead of as the means for its fulfilment. In her journeying Israel encountered temptation; it lay in wait for her at every stage, both in the desert and in Canaan, both under the Kings and after the Exile; and it beset her both in prosperity and in adversity.

The tradition about the Hebrews' attitude on the morrow of the Exodus is revealing in this connection. No sooner has Israel left Egypt than she began to hanker for the past. The land of Pharaoh imposed a burdensome servitude upon her, to be sure, but it offered her security; if it was a slave's existence yet it was a safe one. The chosen people had been the merest apprentices when it came to knowing the liberty Yahweh had obtained for them and they did not know what to do with it because of their fear of dying in the desert. To God's initiative they answered with murmurings; and they preferred food and shelter to independence.

The Hebrews had to learn to rely on none save the God who had snatched them from the Egyptian yoke, to receive from him the manna needed for their existence and to leave it to him to determine the stages of their journey in the desert They wanted to organize themselves and amass wealth so that they need no longer depend constantly on a God who was at once near and elusive, welcoming and inaccessible; they demanded a strong, glorious, visible God, a God to suit their own tastes, who would go before them (Ex. xxxii). To be the people of Yahweh meant willingness to be sustained from moment to moment solely by divine grace alone, to receive everything and merit nothing, to go forward by faith and not by sight, to rely on God and on him alone day after day. The complaints which mark out the stages of Israel's history in the desert show how the chosen people reacted to temptation.

Temptation awaited Israel in the Promised Land, which was also the Land of Canaan, where Baal was sovereign. To safeguard their future the Israelites, as we saw, were prepared to go so far as to worship him. To be sure they did not deny what they owed to Yahweh for the past, but they believed their present existence to depend on the Canaanite god, who must therefore be handled carefully (Hosea I–III: Kings XVIII). Another temptation lay in wait for the Chosen People; that of imitating the surrounding states in order to become a great power. Israel demanded a king; it was no longer enough for her to have Yahweh as monarch; did not any nation worthy of the name have a court and soldiers and diplomats? So the Chosen People, who could no longer count on the power and wisdom of their God, had to have them. The politicians and military leaders were to dictate to Israel what her attitude should be and to involve her in military and diplomatic adventures, and Yahweh's people were to sell their political and religious independence in order to take part in the game of alliances that were to drag her along the road of compromise. The interests of the state demanded it; thus it was appropriate that the God of Israel should become accommodating and open to reason; more-over, was not the cause of religion one with the national cause? For the authorities in Israel, Yahweh was a tool in the service of the national interest.

Even the Jerusalem Sanctuary became a snare for the Chosen People. It constituted their pride and joy; it assured them of Yahweh's presence in their midst and offered a guarantee against hard times. The worship of Yahweh was regularly celebrated with pomp and splendour in the Holy City; pilgrims flocked to Jerusalem, sacrifices were heaped up on the altar, hymns resounded to the glory of Yahweh. Israel was a religious nation yielding nothing in this regard to her neighbours; her God could count on gifts, libations, whole burnt offerings and prayers! But the people of Yahweh and their priests first and foremost forgot what mattered above all else: their worship of God could not serve as an alibi. Neither the zeal of those officiating nor the ardour of worshippers nor the splendour of the ritual could compensate for immorality and iniquity. Yahweh was incorruptible; he could not be bought. The temple ceremonies were an abomination to him; the noise of their songs did not prevent his hearing the cries of victims despoiled of their rights; the crowd of demonstrators did not conceal from him the blood of the innocent that had been shed (Isa. i; Amos v). Jerusalem thought the sanctuary gave her unconditional protection; her inhabitants were wont to cry " The Temple of the Lord, the Temple of the Lord " (Jer. vii). No misfortune would overtake them since God was dwelling in their midst. But they made a mockery of his laws, despised his commandments and thought only of profiting from their privileges and enjoying their advantages. God's people had ceased to be aware that Yawheh was not a tool for their passions, small or great. To be chosen, implied not permission to live as one liked, but rather a special responsibility (Amos iii.2); it depended on a God who did not authorize either injustice or lustfulness. The great ones of Israel who made use of Yahweh in their own interests were to discover his sovereignty when first Samaria and then Jerusalem were to be delivered into the hands of the enemy coming from the north.

Temptation awaited the faithful Jews even in the solicitude entertained towards the divine Law. After the Exile Israel tried to establish a theocracy; a series of rules and regulations was to safeguard the purity of those who claimed the attention of Yahweh. Ezra imposed the Torah so that God should be worshipped at Jerusalem by a people worthy of him. This effort which was sound in its intention was vitiated in the course of time: the pious considered that their works gave them access to salvation and they despised and condemned those who did not show the same zeal as they did in regard to the Law; they confined Yahweh within a system of strictly retributive justice and identified their ideal of piety with the divine will. There lay in this misapprehension the origin of the conflict between the Pharisees and the Christ sent to Israel to declare to her the whole counsel of God.

God's people encountered temptation in the most diverse forms and yet when all is said the snare was always the same one: that held out to Adam and Eve by the serpent in the Garden of Eden when it perfidiously said " Did God really say? . . . You will not die. . . . You will be like God " (Gen. III.1–6). Would Israel accept herself as the Servant of Yahweh who looks to him for everything, or would she be her own master? Did she intend to safeguard her destiny herself and accomplish her salvation by appropriating the gifts of her God; or was she going to entrust herself to the faithful and efficacious solicitude of Him who called her into life by offering her at once her freedom and the opportunity to serve him. The temptation was to cease having continual resort to Yahweh, but like Adam and Eve to put herself beyond the reach of surprise of every kind—that is, beyond God's reach by the acquisition of knowledge: such temptation is born of incredulity and flourishes in pride. Israel's error reflects that of Adam and Eve, and the " fall " in the Garden of Eden is illustrated and confirmed by the Chosen People's long series of unfaithful acts.

The divine " Nevertheless! "

Is the Covenant history the story of a defeat? One might think so, to run through the pages of the Old Testament. The murmurings of Exodus, the betrayals of the kings, the crimes of Samaria and Jerusalem, the compromises of the priests and the good consciences of Job's friends are all indications of how Israel reacted to the devil's snares. Quite early on, the affair of the golden calf was significant: the chosen people intended to serve God in its own way and the god that suited them. Yahweh was to adapt himself to the interests of his people and his role was to safeguard the national glory. The God of Israel was pushed out of his own abode; he found in the temple a priesthood that had annexed the cult to its own ends; his Law was in the hands of scribes who interpreted it to suit themselves; his people was subject to the court and its high officials, and his land was in fee to Baal. Assuredly Yahweh was constantly mentioned; they invoked him and prayed to him and sang his praises, but neither his promises nor his demands were taken seriously. The Covenant had failed.

Yahweh refused to have it so. He was not resigned to becoming a tool in the hands of his people nor to renouncing his plan for salvation for mankind. He would neither consent to being betrayed by an unfaithful nation, nor to being ignored in the universe. His people was to succeed despite the lapses of Israel.

The prophetic ministry illustrates this twofold intention of God, showing clearly that Yahweh did not shut his eyes to the errors of his people but announcing that through judgement God was coming to establish his rule. Yahweh's ' No ' to the pretensions of the kings, the priests, the diplomats and the pious, testified that in his eyes the Covenant remained in force; He refused to abandon Israel to her temptation, and stood firm over against his faithless partner.

The Israelite prophet has often been misunderstood. He has been changed into a diviner whose task was to predict the future; or into the layman who in opposition to the clergy proclaimed an essentially moral religion; or into the social revolutionary who denounced the injustices of the " haves ", and the plundering of the " have-nots ". . . . More recently he has been regarded as the reformer correcting abuses or as the restorer of authentically Yahwist traditions. . . . In reality the prophet's mission was not to preach a new ideology

63

of whatever kind it might be, but to set his contemporaries once again before God as a person; he brought Israel face to face with Someone, not with a teaching or an ideal; he left Yahweh and his people confronting each other.

This visitation of God, as Scripture calls it, was first of all an indictment against an adulterous nation; Yahweh was conducting a law-suit against his people, in which the verdict was a foregone conclusion. The prophets heaped up proofs of their people's guilt. Israel was condemned because God remained faithful to his Word.

Those who heard the prophets could not believe their ears and refused to admit their dilemma; they were unwilling to take cognizance either of the enormity of their crimes or of the foes God sent upon them. The tragedy of the prophets —from Amos to Jeremiah—and from Isaiah to Ezekiel—was that they were sent to a people that was deaf and blind.

History mercilessly cut down the people of God; the Assyrians, as the rod of divine anger, reduced Samaria to slavery; Nebuchadnezzar, in the role of a servant of Yahweh, conducted a holy war against Judah. The temple was given to the flames, the pagans occupied Jerusalem, and Judah departed into exile.

But the prophetic ministry was not fulfilled with the proclamation of God's judgement. Yahweh's messenger was called to destroy but also to build up, to " overthrow . . . and to plant " (Jer. 1); he reminded his hearers that God's grace persistently kept open a gateway to salvation which sin was striving to shut once and for all. All was not lost because Jerusalem was in ruins and her king had been deported. Yahweh was offering his people a possibility of living on beyond the crisis. " It may be that the Lord . . . will be gracious " says Amos (Amos v.15) and Joel cries " Yet even now . . . return to me " (Joel II.12 ff.). Jeremiah announces that a new Covenant will be sealed between God and his people (Jer. xxxi.31–34); Ezekiel conjures up the idea of Israel's resurrection and II Isaiah preaches that the exiles will be comforted (Isa. xl–lv). God remains free to love and to save in spite of everything.

Yahweh's plan was being accomplished, salvation was becoming a reality and the glory of the God of Israel was being extolled throughout the universe, but the way to this objective led through suffering and humiliation. There is a famous page evoking the tragic destiny of the Servant of Yahweh who goes to be tortured, a target for the scorn of everyone, and who in dying is executed for men's sins: " He was despised, and we esteemed him not. Surely he has borne our griefs and carried our sorrows . . . we esteemed him stricked, smitten by God, and afflicted. But he was wounded for our transgressions, he was bruised for our iniquities . . . and the Lord has laid on him the iniquity of us all . . . he poured out his soul to death . . . he bore the sin of many, and made intercession for the Transgressors " (Isa. liii).

The passion of Christ has given fulness of meaning to this mysterious declaration of the exilic prophet; the Gospel reveals to us that God's faithfulness has led him to give the world his beloved son. God's " nevertheless ! " to the shortcomings of his people is made manifest in " the cross ", " a stumbling-block to Jews and folly to Gentiles, but to those who are called, both Jews and Greeks, Christ the power of God and the wisdom of God " (I Cor. 1.17–25).

V

On Reading the Old Testament

THE previous studies have been a kind of approach to the Old Testament. We first took note of the remoteness that for various reasons separates us from it; and we followed this up trying to move some way towards it. Now we are face to face with it: and since in this we are concerned with the reading of Scripture the question inevitably arises, how we are to set about it.

Here we must say that the difficulties we have raised are not going to vanish automatically; there is no infallible recipe for reading the Old Testament. We have no " Open Sesame " that can eliminate all the obstacles and dispel misapprehensions. Some theologians wrongly give the impression that Scripture has no more problems for them, and that to be surprised by a narrative, to jib at an affirmation, or to experience boredom with a genealogy is to show one's complete lack of understanding of the Bible. Brilliant but insubstantial formulae are to be distrusted and it must be recognized that the Old Testament remains a difficult book. Reading the Bible is like all-in wrestling with the text and with the Holy Spirit—rather after the pattern of Jacob's struggle with the angel (Gen. XXXII); Scripture delivers up its secrets to those who take the time to walk with it; it has nothing to say to the dilettante or the braggart.

It must be added that we are not left to our own resources in the matter of arriving at a proper understanding of the Old Testament: God has put us in the Church so that we can reflect on the sacred text with her; we are together in the school of Scripture and we help each other by our mutual labours and discoveries. Bible-study notes, commentaries, courses, congregational studies, camps and Bible weeks come as a stimulus to our investigations; new translations, atlases, concordances, indices, and even records and films are at our disposal so that progress may be made. It is worth while sustaining the effort. Countless in number are those who have found in the pages of this old book the Word of Life illuminating and transfiguring their existence.

One fact has come across to us from these pages: The Old Testament—and in general the Bible—does not consist of a collection of predictions that were accomplished in due season or are in process of fulfilment. It is not a kind of coded message giving advance information about Israel's destiny or that of the Church, or announcing not just the coming of Christ but also the growth of Islam, the Reformation, the world wars and what not—be it Communism, Hitler or the Vatican Council—as some sects would have it. It is not a code-book which is to be deciphered by dint of certain special revelations.

Neither is the Old Testament a collection of relatively beautiful and edifying stories, such as those of Adam and Eve, Abraham's sacrifice of Isaac, Jacob's being deceived by Laban, Joseph's interpreting dreams, and so on—stories from which we might draw a moral, for instance that Adam and Eve were punished for disobeying, that Jacob was the deceiver deceived, that Solomon's difficulties were proportionate to the number of his wives, and the like. Often the impression we take away from our Sunday School contacts with the Old Testament boils down to this kind of teaching: Israel's

Scriptures seem made up of this type of ill-assorted series of stories and to present us first and foremost with a gallery of examples to be imitated or shunned; it does not truly amount to a history.

Now, as we have said more than once, the Old Testament establishes itself as the echo of a real experience undergone by a historical people in a spatial and temporal context which we now know with some degree of precision. The Old Testament tells of a plan made by God for men which was fulfilled with Israel despite the insufficiency of Yahweh's people; this divine plan in turn concerns us and, as members of the People of God we are heirs of the promises given to the Fathers and of the Law given to Moses—heirs of the Messianic hope that was linked with the kingship of David and heirs of the faith of the prophets, psalmists and sages—we are, as Israel's successors, involved in an enterprise which will be accomplished when God is " all in all " (I Cor. xv.28).

There are various ways of grappling with the Old Testament; each has its own truth and also its own dangers and each can be justified only in so far as it does not claim to be exclusive. The New Testament shows us that it has itself made use of several methods in order to read Scripture; we thus have authority for making use of various complementary ways of reading it.

" Atomistic " Reading

This kind of reading starts from the conviction that the Bible is God's Word; each of its books, of its pages, of its verses even, is inspired by Him who above and beyond the witnesses he employs is the real author of Holy Scripture when all is said—God himself. This is based on the apostle's declaration to Timothy: " All Scripture is inspired by God and profitable for reading, for reproof, for correction and

68

for training in righteousness, that the man of God may be complete, equipped for every good work " (II Tim. III.16 ff., cf. also II Peter 1.21).

This way of understanding the Old Testament consists of fastening on the text of Scripture itself, on the verses and sometimes on one or other verse constituting the primary unit of Scripture, the " atom " (whence the name " atomistic reading "). In this the context of a particular biblical statement is of little account; so too its age, or its geographical, historical or literary position; the essential thing is the fact that it is found in the Bible and that by this very fact it enjoys canonical authority.

The New Testament thus makes use of certain Old Testament affirmations without taking into account their original setting, and gives them a meaning which does not necessarily coincide with the thought of the Israelite author.

In this light the Old Testament appears to be like a kind of reservoir of verses, sacred sayings and divine declarations. Works of devotion invite us to draw from the Bible a collection of verses rich in spiritual content. For instance the annual 'Text Books' published by the Moravian brethren offer their readers a daily motto which is either a promise or an exhortation or a warning and is simply a verse taken from Scripture. We read words such as: " The Lord is my shepherd, I shall not want "; " Go in this thy might "; " Blessed is the man who puts his trust in the Lord "; "I delight in mercy, not sacrifice "; " My son, give me thy heart ", etc.

Numerous Christians have with perfect justification made a habit of underlining in the Bible this or that passage or even verse and of learning by heart a fragment of Scripture such as Pss. XXIII, CXXI, and CXXX, and so providing for themselves a sort of treasury—something put by which will nourish their spiritual life.

Nevertheless this atomistic reading is inadequate and it carries with it grave dangers if one aims to leave matters there. It is not enough to quote a biblical text in order to be in the right. All the sects use and abuse this method in order to justify the most eccentric doctrines. There is significance in the fact that it was Scripture the devil used in order to tempt Jesus (Matt. iv.6).

This method leaves entirely out of account the contrasts which the biblical message exhibits; it puts every text on the same level from the mere fact of its being found in the Bible. It does not take into serious account the context, which allows us to define precisely the import of the quoted passage; nor does it trouble about the original sense of the biblical terms which it is too often content to churn out repeatedly *ad nauseam*. It disregards the human factor in the development of Holy Scripture, a factor to which God himself has attached great importance since after using men to reveal himself, he came into our midst by his son, Jesus Christ.

There are fundamental pages and secondary pages in Scripture—there are crucial revelations and complementary ones. Thanks to the work of the historians, the archaeologists and the exegetes, the Old Testament appears to us today like some country that has its hills and its valleys, its peaks and its plateaux; it has a theological configuration which has to be taken into account.

With the atomistic method it is possible to maintain anything one likes, whether the truest of theories or the wildest of errors. Has not racial segregation been justified with the help of a verse in Genesis about the curse of Canaan, which has absolutely no bearing on the colour question? It would be simple to justify the most ghastly massacres in the name of Scripture. . . . If it is normal to take some unforgettable texts from the Old Testament, yet there should be no question of being content with a use of the Bible which

70

does not take seriously the fact that God wished to reveal himself through the history of men.

"Historical" Reading

Conversely, a second way of looking at the Old Testament consists in reckoning with the "time" factor. The Scriptures of Israel were not made in a day; its pages reflect a slow process of elaboration, a progressive advance into broad daylight. The message of the Old Testament is to be understood by placing it in its proper time: the time of Promise, or the time of the Advent. The Old Testament faces towards the Christ who is to come and whose name is as yet unknown to it, the New Testament looks to Jesus Christ who has come and it confesses his name and his victory.

As between the writings of the Old Testament and those of the New there is a difference; the perspective is not the same. There is nothing surprising in stating that the apostolic writers are not saying the same as the Old Testament authors.

Jesus himself in the Sermon on the Mount emphasizes this distinction in declaring several times over: "You have heard that it was said . . . but I say to you . . .". Thus we find that he is not afraid to oppose Moses on the question of the law on divorce (Mt. xix.3 ff).

The Resurrection, which plays an essential part in everything the apostolic generation wrote on the morrow of Easter is almost unheard of in relation to the Old Testament. Suffering provokes different reactions in Jeremiah and Job or in Paul; the first two, coming before the Passion, considered themselves deprived of God's presence by the very fact of their distress; the apostle for his part, lives in the most tragic moments of his ministry in complete communion with Christ and knows that nothing—not even death—can separate him from his God (Rom. viii.31–39). The Old

Testament horizon is above all that of a people, a land and a language. The Church gathers together from the very ends of the earth believers of every race and language and age, who confess the glory of Jesus Christ. Between the Old and the New Testaments there has come into being as it were a bursting of the bounds till then imposed by God on the history of his people.

These few recollections invite us to place the Old Testament in its own special context and not to throw everything into confusion by trying to find the entire Gospel of Christ in the pages of the Old Covenant. Between the Old Testament and ourselves there are the cross of Christ and his message; we shall take care not to leave it out of account in considering this vindictive prayer from Israel's psalter or that imprecation uttered in reference to the enemy of the Chosen People.

The Old Testament is witness to a history stretching over more than ten centuries, with its progress and its set-backs, its light and its shade; the Old Testament testifies to the infinite patience of God who trains Israel as a father brings up his child. From crude human clay so similar to ours, God brings out here and there flashes of surprising spiritual intelligence. Each page of the Old Covenant recounts what has been gained and what remains to be done; we must not ask of the men of the Old Testament more than they have received; we have rather to understand fully what they have transmitted.

In this historical perspective one often stops, and rightly, at the principal witnesses of sacred history—the extraordinary figures of Abraham, Moses, David, Elijah etc. It is good to meditate on the narrative of a " call " [1] and to see Elijah getting to grips with Canaanite worship (I K. xvii ff.), or Amos contending with Samaria's unrighteousness (Amos v),

[1] Moses: Ex. iii-iv; Isaiah, Isa. vi; Jeremiah, Jer. i; Ezekiel, Ez. i; Amos, Am. vii.

72

or Isaiah at odds with the policy of Ahaz or Hezekiah (Isa. VII–VIII; XXX–XXXI). We must also hear Jeremiah striving with his people and his God, Job lending his voice to those who are beyond understanding God's activity, the Preacher (Ecclesiastes) as he reduces human existence to its proper proportions, the Song of Solomon, singing of human love, Nehemiah labouring for the cause of God, or the Psalmists teaching us to pray. What variety there is among these witnesses to the Old Covenant—and what riches are in their words; how revitalising and how indispensable their message is!

The danger in this kind of reading is that the Old Testament runs the risk of seeming first and foremost, indeed almost solely, a witness to a past age. The Old Testament as a document of the past, and, one might say, past being useful . . . in these circumstances it is easy to pass judgement on it rather than to give heed to it, or to reject it instead of hearing what it has to say. With what ease we emphasize the contrasts between the Old Covenant and the New; we oppose the Law to the Gospel, the God of justice to the God of grace, the book of wrath to the book of forgiveness. . . . We make a point of the God of hosts who delivers up populations to be massacred and takes vengeance on Edom and Egypt, in order to exalt the Father of the parable of the prodigal son and the attitude of Christ as he pardons his executioners on the cross. By way of sweeping asseverations we reject in fact, if not in theory, the Old Testament message. How many people treat it as a poor relation, or an embarrassing witness to a past that is gone for ever?

Marcion, early in the history of the Church, openly demanded the suppression of the Jewish documents in the Christian canon. Many of our contemporaries lack his frankness, but would like us to give up mentioning the Old Testament or to talk about it as little as possible. To some theologians its one merit is to testify to the superiority of the Christian revelation! According to some other Christians, only extracts from the Old Testament should be published. The availability of select passages in published form can be justified from the educational standpoint; however it cannot replace direct contact with the entirety of the sacred Scriptures of the Jewish people and the nascent Church. The Old Testament passed on to the New a sacred history, a terminology and a set of ideas and themes which do not assume their true meaning except when set once more in the total context of the biblical documents.

A " historical " reading of the Old Testament runs the risk of turning it for modern readers into the witness of another age—a museum-piece that can interest those with a love for the past; it does not take into account the rich topicality of its message.

Typological Reading

Another way of reading the Old Testament, for which there are precedents in the New Testament, the early Fathers, and also the Reformers, consists in tracing the lineaments of the face of Christ in the many faces of the Old Testament and recognizing, in the diversity of events that it records a prophecy of the Saviour's destiny and work. In his reading of Holy Scripture, Luther was primarily interested in what concerned Jesus Christ. He looked for Christ in the pages of the Old and the New Testaments alike, and did not like in particular the letter of James and the book of Esther because he had been unable to discern the Son of God in these writings.

The apostolic writers draw parallels between the person and work of Christ on the one hand and certain persons, institutions and events in the Old Testament; they emphasize the points of contact between the two parts of Scripture, and without denying moreover what is new in the Gospel. The Old Testament offered them a whole collection of types of Christ (hence the name " typological "). It proclaimed in outline, as it were, what was to be fulfilled by him. The writings of the Old Covenant facilitate these comparisons when they promise the coming of a new David, the conclusion of a second covenant, the possibility of another Exodus, thus relating the events and personages of the past (especially those of the period of the departure from Egypt) to the events and personages of the " end of the ages ".

In John's Gospel, the desert manna appears as a sort of prefiguration of the Bread of Life; the serpent lifted up in the wilderness is a prophecy of the lifting up of the Son of Man on the Cross, and the death of the paschal lamb is compared with the sacrifice of Christ. In connection with his ministry Jesus alludes to Jonah, Solomon and David, and as he dies cites Psalm XXII, while Matthew sees his work as the fulfilment of Isaiah LII. The temptations of Jesus in the desert recall those of the people of Israel as they journeyed towards the Promised Land. Paul compares Christ's function with that of Adam and in Peter's letters the theme of the Flood is bound up with the sacrament of baptism. . . . In brief, the apostolic writers were sensitive to the existence of parallels between the Old Testament on the one hand and the deeds, words and destiny of their Master and his Church on the other. This they expressed variously in their writings. Before intervening through his Son, God contrived that his witnesses of the Old Covenant should somehow sketch out the great work that Christ was to accomplish.

The Church Fathers were to prolong and develop this typological reading which has for some years now been used again by some theologians with varying degrees of success. This type of reading insists on the unity of the biblical message; all interest is focused on Christ and on his body which is the Church: Abraham, Joshua, Solomon and the other Old Testament witnesses come in simply to portray Christ by their actions, their statements, or their circumstances. The men of the Old Covenant are then no longer remote from us; with Kierkegaard we can see ourselves as the contemporaries of the patriarchs, prophets and sages of Israel. The sacrifice of Israel confronts us with the gift of another beloved Son; the desert wanderings suggest the situation of the Church on earth; the passage of the Red Sea or of the Jordan illuminates the meaning of Christian baptism; Joshua heralds a second Joshua—Jesus of Nazareth (the names " Joshua " and " Jesus " are the same).

Typological or christological reading of the Old Testament allows us to find an immediate point of contact with its pages. Thanks to this nearness recovered for us outside the sphere of critical and historical studies, the Old Covenant's writings are again of concern for the people of the New Covenant.

The danger in this kind of reading is that it can degenerate into a sort of ingenious game in which free rein is given to allegory; under the pretext of emphasizing the unity of the biblical message we then fail to recognize its diversity. The topicality of the Old Testament is stressed without any care for what the sacred writers really thought; one's own particular theology is brought into the study of the texts; more virtuosity and imagination is exhibited than deep knowledge of the Old Testament. The crossing of the desert becomes the figure for the spiritual pilgrimage of the soul; Moses' marriage with the foreign woman represents the union of faith with profane culture; the creation of Eve is a type of the resurrection of the flesh; the red heifer predicts the passion of Christ; the scarlet thread used by Rahab, the harlot of Jericho, refers to Christ's blood ensuring the salvation of mankind . . . there is no reason to stop and preachers are to be found who juggle with the texts under the pretext of typological exegesis.

To use the Old Testament in such a way as this is to deny its specific message since the Gospel must then inevitably be already found in it before its time. History is spurned and the real meaning of words is regarded as unimportant, for the comparisons often depend on a mere detail of the text. God had walked for more than ten centuries with his people but there is hardly a care for this, since all Scripture is focused on a single point: the coming of Jesus Christ and his work.

Like the historical type of reading, typological reading taken to the extreme contains its own condemnation. The one accentuates the diversity of the biblical message to the detriment of its unity; the other passes to a concentration on Christology and neglects the variety in Scripture. The former tends to relegate the Old Testament to the past; the latter makes it topical in such a way as to blur the different stages of sacred history. Typologists tend to sniff at history and its implications, while historians are apt to overlook the fact that God's past interventions have kept a permanent significance for the generations of the present. Each of these methods has, in addition to its own particular truth, an element of error that can lead to a denial of the Old Testament and of the biblical revelation.

Theological Reading

It remains to indicate another way of reading the Old Testament, which, without excluding the three we have just expounded, seeks to take the witness of the books of the Old Covenant seriously as one of the constitutive elements of Scripture.

This involves understanding the text and letting it speak for

77

itself as much and as well as possible. This kind of reading implies genuine and deep exegesis of the passage offered for examination and meditation; the essential components of this passage, its origin, structure and place in the context of the book to which it belongs and its position in the setting of the Old Covenant—all these are so many indispensable hints for understanding it properly; and to this study must be added naturally an investigation of the historical, literary and geographical context etc. The aim is to get at the specific message of the text studied—to find its theological kernel. We have to discover what is theologically at stake in a page of the Old Testament—what God is saying to his people through it. It is by understanding the message addressed to the people of the Old Testament that as members of the New Covenant we shall be instructed in the Word of God. We read Israel's Holy Scriptures confidently because Christ was brought up on them and because he both confirmed them and brought them to perfection; we meditate on them alongside and together with the Gospel of Christ.

Having once heard, it remains to respond. The application must not come prematurely; let us not be hasty in averring that we have understood scripture. Our response will be discovery, not imitation. Israel's example was not given to us to be copied but so that we might discover with its help what God expects from us today. The question of discovery is indeed a very real one here, with the unknown element of risk implied in that term. The life of faith is an adventure and not servile submission to the letter of a text. Holy Scripture which from Genesis to the Gospel proclaims our liberation does not aim at tying us to formulae of the past; it calls upon us to be grown, responsible beings.

Why, then, when all is said, do we read the Old Testament and the Bible? Not in the first instance in order to acquire a good Protestant conscience which after the example of our forebears makes us do our daily duty in the shape of contemplating a passage of the Sacred Book; nor in order to know by heart a certain number of verses in order to brandish them as irrefutable arguments in the faces of those of Roman Catholic, sectarian or atheistic persuasion who contradict our position; nor yet to look there for a sensational revelation so as to know the immediate future of our planet and the fate held in store for us. We do not open the Scripture solely to find there an encouragement, an exhortation or a warning; we do not pause at the Old Testament just to satisfy our historical curiosity and to plumb the past of the people of God; we do not meditate on the pages of the Old Covenant essentially in order to discern in it a parable of the work and person of Christ; we read the Bible and particularly the Old Testament in order to hear a word which transforms us, to acquire what might be termed a biblical mentality, to become spiritual Semites in the midst of a generation which feels and thinks outwith the biblical categories and even against the scriptural revelation. There must be formed in us a biblical way of looking at man and the world; in our day we need Christians who possess a sort of biblical sensitivity, and who by long practice in the use of Scripture have acquired "biblical reflexes", that is, who confronted by the problems of our time, react like men of the Bible.

This biblical foundation which is necessary for our behaviour in the world is equally necessary in ecumenical dialogue, in the encounter within the Church of Christians with differing mentalities who belong to alien or even mutually hostile cultures. There is need in the Church of the twentieth century for Christians from Asia, Africa, Europe and America who have assimilated Scripture to the point of having acquired a "biblical consciousness" which will permit them to understand and to help each other.

Now, there can be no improvisation in this sphere; one

does not become a " biblical man " all at one go, but rather by a sustained effort and in prolonged contact with Scripture as a whole.

On a great variety of points the contribution of the Old Testament corrects distortions which there is a risk of provoking in the Church by reading focussed on the Gospel.

The Old Testament has a sensitivity towards God and it reacts by its theocentric message to those ways of preaching salvation whose sole objective is the satisfaction of the individual soul. To the more or less latent egocentricity of a certain type of revivalism the Old Testament opposes its vision of the divine work which reaffirms God's glory and the transfiguration of the universe. Christ did not die on the cross just for our spiritual afflictions, but in order to lay the foundation for a new humanity, a new heaven and a new earth.

The Old Testament is interested in history; it exhibits God's vigilance in regard to the nation and their behaviour; it gives meaning to the passage of time and reveals that all mankind is journeying towards an encounter with God. The God of Jesus Christ is not solely concerned with the salvation of souls; nothing that goes on here in this world escapes his providence; politics are also the concern of his judgement and his grace.

The Old Testament tells us of God's solicitude to ensure the defence of the small, the unprivileged, the poor; the Law of Moses and the interventions of the prophets (Amos, Isaiah, Jeremiah) alike indicate that the God of Israel champions the oppressed and does not tolerate the despoiling of men. An entire social and even economic ethic can be extracted from Israel's writings and can inform our discussion in these spheres.

The Old Testament breathes life and fulness and demands a form of worship worthy of God; the songs of the Chosen

People were renowned as far as Babylon and the imposing and minutely detailed descriptions of the construction of the Tabernacle are a record of preoccupation with this, which has no room for the attitude of " second best will do ", or for the slovenly work and the sketchiness which satisfy us as soon as our concern is with the things of God.

The writings of the Old Testament have many things to teach the Church concerning Jesus Christ, or of which to remind it, whether on the value of each creature, made in the image of God, or on war and peace, or on sin and forgiveness, or on love and justice.

Chronological Outline of the History of the Chosen People

1. *The Hebrews: the Patriarchal Age.*

Century B.C.	Hebrew History	Contemporary Events
19		Egyptian Middle Kingdom
18	ABRAHAM	Babylon: Hammurabi
		Westward migration of Semitic tribes
		Hyksos invasion of Egypt
	Hebrews in Egypt	
15		Egypt: 18th dynasty
		(Tell el-Amarna)
		Hittite Empire
14		Egypt: 19th Dynasty
		Egypt: Seti I
13		Ramses II (ca. 1300–1234)
	MOSES: Exodus: Covenant	
	JOSHUA: in Canaan (ca. 1225)	Egypt: Menephtah

2. The Israelites: the period of the Kings and the Prophets

Century B.C.	Hebrew History	Contemporary Events
		The Sea Peoples
12	The Judges	Philistines in Palestine
11	SAUL: first King of Israel	
	DAVID: conquers Philistines ★	
	(ca. 1000)	
	SOLOMON: builds Temple	
10	Split between *Israel* and *Judah* (932)	
9	OMRI's Dynasty:	Rise of Assyria
	OMRI (in Samaria)	
	AHAB	
	The prophet ELIJAH	Shalmaneser III
		Damascus threatens Israel
	Coup d'état by JEHU (842)	
8	JEROBOAM II of Israel:	743 onwards: Tiglath-pileser III intervenes in west
	Prophets in Israel: AMOS	
	HOSEA	
		732 Fall of Damascus,
	Judah: Kings AHAZ	721 of Samaria (under Sargon II)
	HEZEKIAH	711 Fall of Ashdod (Sennacherib)

★ See previous reference in other column.

83

Century B.C.	Hebrew History	Contemporary Events
8	Judah: Prophets: ISAIAH MICAH Samaria disappears ★ Last-minute deliverance of Jerusalem (701)	
7	Manasseh and Amon: vassals of Assyria Prophets: ZEPHANIAH NAHUM Political and religious restoration Deuteronomic reform (622) under JOSIAH (died 609) Prophetic ministry of JEREMIAH Prophet HABAKKUK?	612 Fall of Nineveh (Assyrian capital) Pharaoh Neco II defeats JOSIAH Neco is defeated by the Babylonians
6	JEHOIAKIM revolts against Nebuchadnezzar and is defeated ★ First deportation (597) ZEDEKIAH revolts Second deportation (587) End of the state of Judah	After 605: Nebuchadnezzar master of the Middle East

★ See previous reference in other column.

84

Century B.C.	Hebrew History	Contemporary Events
		Cyrus of Persia
	EZEKIEL among the exiles " II ISAIAH " among the exiles	538 Fall of Babylon Edict of Cyrus
	Return to Palestine under Zerubbabel* Oracles of HAGGAI, ZECHARIAH Temple rebuilt (520–515)	Period of Darius Wars of the Medes
4	Prophet MALACHI Political & religious restoration under NEHEMIAH and EZRA (ca. 458–397) Establishment of *Judaism* Oracle of OBADIAH (?)	Victories of Alexander the Great (334–323)
3	Prophets: JOEL (?) " II ZECHARIAH " The Jews under the Ptolemies ★	" Ptolemies " in Egypt Growth of Jewish colony at Alexandria. Hellenistic period in Middle East. Greek translation of Old Testament (Septuagint: " LXX ")

★ See previous reference in other column.

85

Century	Hebrew History	Contemporary Events
B.C.		
2	The Jews under the Seleucids (Syria)	198: Antiochus III the Great defeats Ptolemaic Egypt
	Strife between Hellenizers and their opponents at Jerusalem. Persecution & martyrdoms	Roman intervention. Antiochus Epiphanes (175–164)
	Revolt of Mattathias. Victory of JUDAS MACCABAEUS (165)	
	Book of DANIEL	
	Independent Jewish State (142 onwards)	
	JOHN HYRCANUS (134–104)	
1	Hasmonean Dynasty (from 104):	
	ARISTOBULUS I	
	ALEXANDER JANNAEUS etc.	
	Conflict with Pharisees	
		Roman intervention
	Pompey takes Jerusalem (63)	
	HEROD the Great proclaimed King (37–4)	Palestine under Roman Rule

86

Appendix II

Outline of the Growth of the Old Testament

1. BEFORE THE MONARCHY (till 1000 B.C.)

Period of Oral Tradition.

A great variety of traditions was passed on orally among the Hebrews. At the close of this period they began to form cycles of tradition and they were generally associated with a sanctuary.

To this era belong also the first written documents, which were of cultic origin and included juridical texts like the Ten Commandments.

2. FROM THE BEGINNING OF THE MONARCHY TO ITS CLOSE (to the sixth Century).

Creative Period in Israelite Literature

The principal times of the birth and development of Israelite literature were in the period of David and Solomon, then under Hezekiah, and finally under Josiah.

Tenth–Ninth Centuries:

Official texts.
First collections of psalms and proverbs.
Historiography of the Davidic house.

Yahwistic synthesis of sacred history; first sketch of the Pentateuch, followed by the Elohistic tradition.
Elijah Cycle.

About the Eighth Century:

Progress of the Wisdom Literature and of lyrical writings. First collections of prophetic writings, consisting of the oracles of Isaiah, Amos, Hosai and Micah.
Outline of the Deuteronomic tradition.

Seventh and Sixth Centuries:

Spread of Deuteronomic thinking (Deuteronomy).
Collection of the oracles of Zephaniah and Habakkuk.
First " prophetic " book: Jeremiah.

3. FROM THE EXILE TO THE ROMAN PERIOD (to the First Century B.C.).

Fixing of Jewish Tradition

During this period the cultic, juridical, wisdom, historical and prophetic traditions were preserved and given their final shape; the books of the Old Testament came into being in fixed form. At the same time two new literary categories appeared: edifying writing (midrashes) and apocalyptic. Three points of time stand out: the Exile, the restoration under Nehemiah and Ezra, and the meeting of Judaism and the Hellenistic world.

Sixth Century:

During the Exile the Jews displayed an intense literary activity:

(a) prophecy was represented by Ezekiel and II Isaiah; history by the deuteronomic work on the history of the people of God;

(b) lyrical products were represented by the collection of Lamentations and various Psalms;

(c) legislation was represented by the publication of priestly Laws.

After the Exile:

Following the ministries of Haggai, Zechariah (I–VIII) and, later, Malachi, Ezra rearranged the priestly tradition and made possible the compilation of the Pentateuch (ca. 400 B.C.).

Under Alexander and his successors:

The Prophetic tradition came to an end with Joel and " II Zechariah " (Zech. IX–XIV), and edificatory literature developed in Ruth, Jonah, and, later, Esther, Tobit etc. The Chronicler wrote his historical synthesis. Books in the category of Wisdom Literature appeared, such as Job (ca. 300), Ecclesiastes and Ecclesiasticus (200).

Before the encounter with the Hellenistic world, the prophetic books, the Psalter and Proverbs had been completed. The crisis under Antiochus Epiphanes in the Second century B.C. made possible the development of Apocalyptic, of which the book of Daniel is the official representative alongside non-canonical documents such as the book of Enoch and the Testaments of the Twelve Patriarchs.

Appendix III

Some Manuscripts of Importance for establishing the Old Testament Text

HEBREW DOCUMENTS

Nash Papyrus. This contains only the decalogue and the " Shema Israel " (cf. Deut. VI.4 ff); it is a liturgical text found about 1900 A.D. and dating from just before the Christian era.

Manuscript of Isaiah (1 Q Is^a), discovered in 1947 near Qumran. This contains an almost complete text of Isaiah which is older than the Christian era.

Manuscript of Samuel (4 Q Sam^b). This comprises important fragments of the book of Samuel and would seem to be one of the oldest known biblical manuscripts, together with a fragment of Exodus (4 Q Ex^f): specialists date it in the third century B.C.

Leningrad Prophets Codex (P.) This consists of the few prophetic books (Isaiah, Jeremiah, Ezekiel and the Twelve Prophets), copied in 916 A.D. The original Babylonian pointing has been replaced by that of Tiberias, which later came into general use.

Leningrad Codex (L or 19a). This was copied in 1008 A.D. through the industry of Aaron Ben Moshe ben Asher, of the renowned family of Massoretes: It comprises the entire Old

Testament and, together with the Aleppo Codex, is the earliest complete manuscript known to us. It was the basis for the critical edition of the Hebrew text (Biblica Hebraica, Third Edn., R. Kittel).

Greek Documents

Papyrus 458. This is one of the oldest Greek documents for the Old Testament. It belongs to the John Rylands Library (Manchester) and dates from the second century B.C. It contains some fifteen verses from Deuteronomy.

Codex Vaticanus (B). This is in the Vatican Library and dates from the fourth century A.D. It contains all the Old Testament apart from some fragments of Genesis, Samuel, and Psalms, and it includes almost the entire New Testament. Together with the *Codex Sinaiticus* (S or ℵ), of the same period, and the fifth century *Codex Alexandrinus* (A) it is one of the first witnesses of the Greek tradition to contain the whole of the Holy Scripture.

Latin Documents

Codex Lugdunensis. This has a Latin text prior to the work of Jerome, and has a seventh century dating.

Codex Amiatinus. This came from Great Britain and belongs to the eighth century. It reproduces the text of the Vulgate in a sixth century revision: it will be remembered that the Vulgate, completed in 405 by Jerome, became the official version of the Roman Church (1592 edition).

Appendix IV

Some Practical Suggestions

1. It is best not to become acquainted with Scripture through the medium of the Old Testament in the first instance. It is preferable to come to the Old Testament books by way of the Gospels and Epistles. There is some value in following a planned syllabus for reading.

2. Passages that strike the reader may profitably be underlined and jotted down in a note-book as a sort of pocket companion.

3. Tracts, commentaries, annotated editions with introductions, and lectionaries are available and there is a growing number of conferences and retreats devoted to the subject, not to mention periodicals. There should be participation in this biblical revival, for the Bible is the book of the people of God and must be read in communion with them.

4. A variety of approaches to the Old Testament is a good thing:

   (a) one may take an interest in Israel's history, consult archaeological works and place the facts in their proper period and geographical location in order the better to understand their message;

   (b) for the New Testament and the Early Fathers one may observe the connection God has established between his former deeds and what he does now, underlining the unity of the biblical witness as it focuses on the work of Christ;

(c) it is always useful to find out how Christian traditions other than our own read and understand, or in the past have read and understood, Scripture.

5. The psalms can be read as prayers—orally on occasions, and antiphonally. Israel's prayers teach us to speak in our turn both to God and of him.

6. Suggestions for further study.
   (a) A series of psalms:

   e.g. praise (Ps. CXLVIII);
         gratitude (Ps. CIII);
         confidence (Ps. XIII);
         repentance (Ps. LI)

   or,

   creation (Ps. CIV);
   God's immeasurable greatness (Ps. CXXXIV);
   the Messiah (Ps. II);
   the human situation (Ps. VIII);
   the coming of God (Ps. XCVI):

   (b) a connected study of the first twelve chapters of Genesis, which deal with the beginning of things, and explain the relations that exist between the Creator, the creature and creation;

   (c) an examination of some chapters of Exodus which narrate the journeyings of the chosen People " from servitude into service ": Ex. I–V; XII–XV; XVI–XVIII; XIX, XX; XXIV; XXXII–XXXIV:

   (d) study of a prophetic book such as Jeremiah, or of the dialogues in Job, or of the reign of David, the memoirs of Nehemiah, etc.;

   (e) Scripture may be usefully skimmed in search of material relating to some central theme, e.g.

   " calls ": Abraham, Moses, Isaiah, Peter, Paul;
   faith: Abraham, Isaiah, Romans IV, Hebrews XI;

suffering: Jeremiah, Job, Psalms (XXII, LXIX), Isaiah LIII, the Passion, Paul;

the wilderness: Exodus, Numbers, Elijah (I K.XIX), Hosea (II), John the Baptist, Jesus;

justice: Isaiah I, Amos V, Micah V, Jeremiah VII, Isaiah LVIII, Matthew XXV.

Bibliography*

The Oxford Annotated Bible (Revised Standard Version), ed. H. G. May and B. M. Metzger. Oxford University Press, 1962.

ALBRIGHT, W. *The Archaeology of Palestine.* Pelican Book, 1954. *From the Stone Age to Christianity.* Second edn. 1957.

ALLMEN, J. J. v. (ed.). *Vocabulary of the Bible.* Lutterworth, 1958.

ANDERSON, B. W. *The Living World of the Old Testament,* Longmans, Green & Co., 1958.

ANDERSON, G. W. *A Critical Introduction to the Old Testament,* Duckworth, 1959.

BALY, D. *The Geography of the Bible.* Lutterworth, 1957.

BLACK, M. & ROWLEY, H. H. (eds.), *Peake's Commentary on the Bible.* 2nd edn., Nelson, 1962.

CORSWANT, W. *Dictionary of Life in Bible Times,* (tr. A. Heathcote), Hodder & Stoughton 1960.

HENTON DAVIES, G. & RICHARDSON, A. (eds.). *The Teacher's Commentary* (Revised), S.C.M. Press Ltd., 1955.

EHRLICH, E. L. *A Concise History of Israel,* (tr. J. Barr) Darton, Longmans & Todd, 1962.

FINEGAN, J. *Light from the Ancient Past.* Princeton, 1946.

GRANT, F. C. & ROWLEY, H. H. (eds.), *Hastings' Dictionary of the Bible.* 2nd edn., T. & T. Clark, 1963.

GRAY, J. *Archaeology and the Old Testament World.* Nelson, 1962.

GROLLENBERG, L. H. *Atlas of the Bible,* tr. & edd. J. M. H. Reid and H. H. Rowley) Nelson, 1956.

JACOB, E. *Theology of the Old Testament* (tr. A. Heathcote), Hodder & Stoughton, 1958.

KUHL, C. *The Prophets of Israel* (tr. R. J. Ehrlich and J. P. Smith), Oliver & Boyd, 1960.

* The French book-list has been somewhat altered. The bibliography is of course by no means exhaustive.

MILLER, M. S. & J. L. *Bible Dictionary*. Seventh edn. A. & C. Black, 1962.

NOTH, M. *History of Israel*. Second edn. (tr. P. R. Ackroyd), A. & C. Black, 1960.

PRITCHARD, J. B. *Ancient Near Eastern Texts Relating to the Old Testament*, 2nd edn., Oxford, 1954.

RAD, G. V. *Theology of the Old Testament*, vol. I, (tr. D. M. G. Stalker) Oliver & Boyd, 1962.

RICHARDSON, A. (ed.), *A Theological Word Book of the Bible*. S.C.M. Press Ltd., 1950.

S. C. M. PRESS LTD., *The Layman's Bible Commentaries*.
The Torch Bible Commentaries.
Studies in Biblical Archaeology. (Vols. by A. Parrot on Nineveh Samaria, the Temple, etc.), 1955.

SMITH, J. W. D. *The Pattern of Christian Belief*. Nelson, 1955.
Bible Background. Methuen, 1959.

WINTON THOMAS, D. (ed.). *Documents from Old Testament Times*. Nelson, 1958.

WRIGHT, G. E. & TOMES, R. *An Introduction to Biblical Archaeology*. Duckworth, 1960.